LEADING
THE
TEAM
WITHIN

Overcoming Challenges and Making Decisions with Confidence by Mastering Self-Leadership

Key lessons, insights, and strategies from your favorite animals supporting you in turning negative self-talk and limiting beliefs into new mindsets and habits transforming you into the successful leader you're destined to be.

"If an egg is broken by outside force life ends. If broken by inside force life begins. Great things always begin from the inside."

Unknown

ANN M. WRIGHT

Leading the Team Within: Mastering Self-Leadership

Copyright 2023 © Ann M. Wright. All rights reserved.

For more information, email Ann at ann@annwrightsolutions.com

ISBN: 979-8-89109-741-4 - paperback
ISBN: 979-8-89109-742-1 - ebook
ISBN: 979-8-89109-743-8 - hardcover
ISBN: 979-8-89316-301-8 - audiobook

Special Thanks

To my husband, Doug.

Your love and unwavering support throughout life and this entire writing and publishing journey has been and continues to be incredible as well as appreciated. I'm so grateful for the life we have and continue to build together.

To my son, Noah.

You are the only one in this entire world who calls me Mom and by far, the greatest blessing in my life. Your sense of humor, kind heart, and generous spirit inspire me each and every day. I love you more than words can say.

Let's Connect!

Thank you so much for deciding to invest in yourself and allowing me to walk this journey with you. To say thanks, please visit my website at www.annwrightsolutions.com/freegift to receive your gift, a worksheet to support you in moving forward with your dreams and goals.

Got Advice for Our College Grads?

If you would like to provide some advice or tips in being successful in life for new or recent college graduates, please go to www.annwrightsolutions.com/advice to share your thoughts. You will receive credit for your contribution if they are included in my next book which will be written in collaboration with my son.

Table of Contents

Letter to My Readers

"What Lies Behind Us Is Nothing Compared To What Lies Within Us And Ahead of Us."

Stephen Covey

Are you wondering why in the world you bought yet another book about leadership? I'm guessing it's because, like me, you're all about becoming the best leader and the best version of yourself that you can be. At times I wondered whether or not it was worth writing yet another book about leadership, because I was challenged on how to make it different from the others. My goal was to make this book inspirational, informational, practical, thought-provoking, and most of all...fun. It's my hope it ends up being all of this and more.

You may wonder: how is this book different from the others? It talks about learning to lead the team on the inside, so you can lead the one on the outside. It shares insight into how all of us can learn to lead our inner team that supports us in our thoughts and actions. It also talks about how we can lead and work with others in our personal and professional life. It focuses on some of the areas that most of us face and are challenged with at some point in our lives. These include confidence, procrastination, times when we are unsure of which decisions to make, goal setting, conflict resolution, distractions, and self-care. It contains stories, lessons learned, strengths, questions to ponder, a place for you to reflect, space to determine your action plan, and additional resources you may want to research.

This book is meant to support you where you are, figuring out where you want to be, how to get there, and planning what you are willing and able to do to get where you want to be. It's about what we can learn from a team, who in my opinion got it right—the geese. You'll meet their team, which includes: the elephant, the rabbit, and the squirrel.

Each and every one of you is a leader. You don't have to have a specific title to be a leader. You can lead a team, a group of peers, your family, volunteers, and yourself. I realized to be a strong leader, parent, and friend, I needed to figure out how to lead myself before I could support others in leading themselves. The information in this book is meant to support you in leading yourself as well as others. It's not a book about theory. It's not about telling you what to do or not to do.

It's up to you to decide what type of leader, friend, parent, spouse, and person you want to be and how you want to lead your team. Some may say there isn't a right or wrong way. That's a tough one for me. I think some ways of leading are more effective, more inspiring, and more successful than others. We have a choice on how to lead ourselves and how to lead others. This is about giving you a place to think about what can work for you.

By the way, I'm a work in progress, just like everyone else. I've learned a lot and still have a lot to learn. In fact, if you have some ideas or lessons you've learned from reading this book, your life experiences, or questions you would like to see explored on my future Podcast or in a future book you can send them to me at wrightsolutions123@msn.com. I am planning to collaborate with my son, Noah, on my next book and we will be seeking out ideas to share with those who are about to graduate or recently graduated from college and are embarking on their journey into the workplace.

I love Dr. Phil's saying, *"You can't change what you don't acknowledge."* Acknowledging something we want or need to improve isn't a sign of weakness, but a sign of courage, self-awareness, and strength.

Thanks for having the courage to explore some areas with which we are all challenged at some point in time. Enjoy the journey and maybe ask someone to join you in experiencing this journey with you. Most of all, have fun. Thank you for allowing me to walk this journey with you. After all, life really is a journey and not a destination.

Wishing you all the best in life,

Ann

About This Book

"Man cannot discover new oceans unless you have the courage to lose sight of the shore."

Andre Gide

Ever feel like you have a million people or things pulling you in different directions? Do you work with a team whom you enjoy being around, and yet you're still trying to figure out how to work with all the different styles and personalities? I feel like this too. Daily.

Having worked on or with teams most of my life, I work to appreciate what each person on the team has to offer. But then again, I'm still human, so I have to consciously remember this when the person is driving me crazy. It really does take a village to support us in all areas of our lives. Aristotle once stated, "the whole is greater than the sum of all parts." It refers to the importance of synergy.

While having conversations with some of my peers, we got talking about some of the things that show up almost daily, both in the workplace and in our personal lives. For some reason, we related them to animals. Where this came from, I have no idea. You know, the elephant in the room who visits us when there's an issue to be addressed but no one really wants to talk about it, the two rabbits we chase and if we chase both of them, each will get away, and then one of my all-time favorites, our beloved squirrel brain.

You know those times when you're working on one thing and then an idea or task pops up and you're off to thinking about or working on something totally unrelated to what you originally were working on? You know how it feels to be excited about a goal or project, get started only to be distracted with other ideas, or allow procrastination to creep into the mix and allow an obstacle to get in your way? I know exactly how you feel. This book, for example, I've been thinking about writing it for a couple of years. I would get started with an idea, my squirrel brain distracted me, and I moved onto the next best idea and, well, you know the result.

Everything gets started and nothing gets finished!

I've discovered many of us recognize these traits within ourselves and see them in others as well. So, what can we do about them? We can either let them lead us or we can decide to learn from them as well as lead them. The team within us is a team which we may not think about. They are part of you and are stronger and wiser than you might realize. Many of our peers, friends, and family members may remind us of our different team members. By understanding and valuing ourselves, all sides of ourselves, we can develop a deeper appreciation not only of ourselves but also of others around us and the value they bring.

Some characteristics are amazing and serve us well, while others can derail us from where we want to go and what we want to accomplish *if* we let them. Each can bring value depending on how you look at it. If we lead and manage them, they can support us in achieving our goals, even if at first it doesn't feel like it.

I decided to name some of those characteristics, which are most likely part of your inner leadership team, too. If we learn how to lead ourselves, we can also lead others.

Usually when people think of a team, we only see the variety of people who make up the team on the outside. This book deals with a different team, the one on the inside of you; the "members" or traits with which we all can identify and have most likely experienced and continue to experience. Some traits we may not like and yet they provide us with a certain value if we look at them from a different lens. Each has different strengths and ideas, even if at first glance we don't see it.

Some of our team members are direct, some inspiring, some calm, some more precise than others. In the beginning I wanted to suppress one of the animals. It's one that I thought was preventing me from moving forward. What I realized is that he was playing a key role in me moving forward. Everyone does bring value to the team and to your team.

Throughout this book I hope you take my humor and kind sarcasm as I mean them, with a grain of salt and fun. I hope you laugh and reflect. This book isn't about me, it's about you. It's a fun and different way to look at the team members that exist within us. If we believe in and appreciate the value we offer and see that all of our internal team members have something to offer, maybe we will begin to see the value others bring to the organization.

Have fun with your "team members" and appreciate that they all have something to offer. You may see many of the team members not only show up in your own life but also within people in the workplace and in your personal life, among family and friends.

I'll share some information about each of our team members, stories about how they work in our lives, lessons learned, and strategies and resources for you to continue exploring the topics in which you're most interested. There will be space for you to take time to reflect on your takeaway(s) from the chapters and make an action plan to use what you've learned if you choose.

My bottom line: I would love to see more people believe in themselves and value the gifts they bring to the world, as well as value what others bring to the world. I think we all would be so much happier and productive in life if we did this.

The inspiration from this book comes from several conversations I had with friends and what they wanted to experience in a book.

Quotes

I love quotes and each chapter shares one or more of my favorite quotes.

Introduction

Each chapter shares information about the strength(s) or the characteristic(s) of each team member even though at first it may seem like a challenge or detriment. You'll meet my "animal" team members, learn how they serve you and me, and how they can distract us if we let them.

Stories

In this section I share one or more stories to show how the "animal" or trait served one of my peers or me well.

Lessons Learned

This section provides you with a summary of the key lessons my friends and I have learned.

Strengths

The animals will share their strengths and you'll have a chance to think about and record your strengths in that area if you choose.

Strategies

At the end of each chapter, there's a list of strategies you can use and may want to try. Choose the one(s) which will best serve you. I encourage you to share them with coworkers, friends, and family. Because in the end, we're all in this together. No one knows everything about anything. Let's learn with and from each other and share as much knowledge as we can to support and help each other be as successful as possible. The strategies included are not an all-inclusive list. They're a place to begin. Feel free to add some of your own.

Your Reflection

Knowledge is great! However, if you don't know how to use it or aren't willing to apply it, it doesn't really do you much good. It doesn't mean you have to put everything you know and have learned into action today. Maybe you tuck it away to use on a rainy day or at a later date, but the important thing is you think about how you might use it today, or in the future. I almost said someday, but someday is not a day of the week. Someday rarely, if ever, comes.

This section is all about you making and taking time to reflect on what you read and journaling those thoughts.

There will be reflection questions for you to ponder and get you started on your reflection. In the college classes I teach, my students have the opportunity—a nice way of saying an assignment—to write reflections. Each reflection contains three questions. The first: what did you learn? The second: what more would you like to learn, or the question you have about the topic? The third: how will or how might you apply what you have learned?

I encourage you to ask yourself some or all of the questions when you're writing your reflection. I've provided a couple of questions to get you started. Let them be a catalyst to get you thinking about the topic if you choose. You don't have to answer all the questions. Heck, you don't have to answer any of them.

Your Biggest Takeaway(s)

This is where you can write your biggest takeaway(s) from the chapter. What do you want to remember and perhaps share with someone else?

Your Action Plan

Like I shared earlier, I'm all about practical application. You don't have to do everything. Yet, I encourage you to do something. Choose whatever it is you would like to work on to be the best you that you can be, and which will support you in living an even more satisfying life. This is the section near the end of each chapter where you can list what you want to work on, what action you'll take to move forward, who could support you in moving forward, when you want to begin, and how you'll know you're making progress.

I encourage you to write something in each chapter but then start with the action from the one chapter that resonates the most with you. In other words, choose one thing to work on and then go back and choose another. It's like I share with my students. How do you eat an elephant? One bite at a time.

Find somewhere that's comfortable where you can take time to think and reflect without distraction when creating your action plan(s).

"Failing to plan is planning to fail."

Attributed to Alan Lakein

Here is an example of what your action plan may look like. I'll include one in each chapter. Remember it's your plan not mine—this is only an example to support you in getting started. Choose the action that will support you in moving forward. There will be space for you to write your personal plan of action at the end of the example.

Example: (this is one from the Rabbit chapter—choosing priorities and setting goals)

1. *Goal: Determine business priorities and goals including action steps and timelines for each.*

2. *Action: Set aside one or two days in July to plan my business goals and priorities for 2024. List each in my calendar with dates and times I will work on them.*

3. *Who will support me? My husband*

4. *Date to begin: May 1, Put dates on calendar. July 17 and 18 develop plan for 2024.*

5. *How will I know I made progress? By the end of the day on July 18, I will have a plan for 2024 listing business priorities with action steps and timeline for 2024.*

Your Turn

1. Goal:
2. Action:
3. Who can support you?
4. Date to begin:
5. How will you know you made progress?

If you ever have a question about an action step, just email me (ann@annwrightsolutions.com) and I'll do the best I can to help.

Self-Assessment

There's a short self-assessment for you to complete if you want to. It's about you assessing where you feel you are currently in the areas discussed. In some you'll be right where you want to be. In others you find there's room to enhance your skills. All of us have room to improve. Some of the areas in which many of us struggle can be strengths if we develop them. The self-assessment is *about* you and *for* you. No one else needs to ever see your results unless you choose to share them. If you decide to use this book with a book club, the reflection questions and assessment may be a great place to begin your discussion. There's one to use before you read the book and one to use after implementing a strategy or two. You can also access a copy of the self-assessment and other resources on my website: annwrightsolutions.com

Additional Resources

This book includes some of my favorite resources on the topics addressed. I encourage you to check them out at your leisure. For example, Simon Sinek has an insightful TED Talk, which focuses on our *Why* (*Start with Why – how great leaders inspire action*). I have watched it several times, and it has helped me keep my focus, especially when the squirrel brain in me still wants and tends to run rampant.

So, whether it's the elephant in the room, the squirrel who chases every shiny object there is, the rabbit who hops about and tempts us to chase too many things at once, or the monkey on your back who shows up, I remind myself there's a leader in every seat and in all my inner team members. Each brings value and has a place on the team. Together we are more successful than we are alone.

Ready to meet the team, see what each brings to the table, and how we can best lead them and utilize their strengths?

Let's do this together!

"Be who you are, not how the world wants you to be."

Unknown

Self-Assessment

*T*his is an opportunity for you to reflect on where you feel you are with regard to topics we are going to talk about in this book before we get started. Remember: no judgment, only a chance to reflect and help yourself determine where your strengths are and where you may want to focus as you continue being the best version of yourself as you lead yourself and help others lead themselves. Everyone is a leader regardless of whether or not you have the "title" of leader. Before we lead others, we need to lead ourselves and the team within us. There is another copy of this at the back of the book you can use in the future as you implement some of the strategies in the areas where you want to elevate your skills.

"You don't have to be great to start but you have to start to be great."

Zig Ziglar

Complete the self-assessment below to see where you believe you are right now with your knowledge and skills. (1 - I could use some work on this. 2 - Sometimes I have it and sometimes I don't. 3 - I got this.)

Characteristic	Self-Assessment		
I can **lead** in situations when appropriate. (Geese)	1	2	3
I am comfortable and **able to follow** someone's lead. (Geese)	1	2	3
I am **able to collaborate** with others. (Geese)	1	2	3
I **accept change** for the most part. (Butterfly)	1	2	3
I am **curious and ask questions.** (Cat)	1	2	3
I am a **patient** person. (Cat)	1	2	3
I am good at **self-care.** (Cat)	1	2	3
I experience **inner peace.** (Dove)	1	2	3
I feel **confident** in most things and in most situations. (Eagle)	1	2	3
I am **able to communicate** with most people. (Elephant)	1	2	3
I am able to **address conflict** in a productive manner. (Elephant)	1	2	3
I have **procrastination** under control. (Monkey)	1	2	3
I am **able to focus** on my priorities/projects. (Ostrich)	1	2	3
I **do not avoid** things that are uncomfortable. (Ostrich)	1	2	3
My **self-talk** is usually positive and serves me well. (Parrot)	1	2	3
I **laugh** and have fun. (Puppy)	1	2	3
I am **loyal.** (Puppy)	1	2	3
I take time to **relax.** (Puppy)	1	2	3
I am able to **make decisions** on what my **priorities** are. (Rabbit)	1	2	3
I am able to **slow down** when appropriate. (Sloth)	1	2	3
I **don't compare** myself to others. (Snake)	1	2	3
I **don't allow fear** to stop me from doing things. (Snake)	1	2	3
I am able to manage my **self-doubt.** (Snake)	1	2	3
I am **not easily distracted.** (Squirrel)	1	2	3
I **manage interruptions.** (Squirrel)	1	2	3
I **persevere** during tough situations. (Tortoise)	1	2	3
I am a **patient** person. (Tortoise)	1	2	3
I gain **wisdom** from mistakes and experiences. (Owl)	1	2	3

The Geese

Lead, Follow, and Collaborate

"Go confidently in the direction of your dreams."

Thoreau

The original plan was for Ann to write this book, yet after a lot of thought, she decided to let our team write the majority of it. I know, at first, it sounded kind of crazy to let a bunch of geese and their friends write a book. After all, you may be thinking, what in the world do noisy geese and a bunch of their animal friends know about you leading yourself, leadership, and collaboration? We asked Ann the same question! Here's the bottom line: this book is about sharing a fun and unique perspective, what each of your inner team members brings to your team. Does it matter which one of us shares the story as long as it supports you? Nope—'cause it's not about her, not about us—it's about you.

This book is about the "members" and the traits with which we can all identify and have most likely experienced and continue to experience. They are characteristics that exist within us and others. Some traits people may not necessarily like and yet they provide them with a certain value if you look at them through a different lens. Each has different strengths and ideas, even if at first glance we don't see it. Just think about how empty and weak our formation would be with only a couple of geese in it, and if we all looked exactly the same. It's just like the team you have within

1

yourself. You are so much stronger because of all the traits you possess even if at first you don't know how in the world they can help you succeed. All of us bring value to the team. Just like all your traits can bring value if you let them and maybe look at them from a different perspective. We're confident you'll be able to identify and relate to our team, as well as, recognize some of the traits your friends on the outside struggle with as they lead their inner team. By the way, it's not about changing you or them, for that matter. It's about capitalizing on the strengths of each.

Do you ever watch a bird and think—wow, how do they fly for so long? Don't their wings get tired? We think the same thing about you—how do you walk, stand, swim, or bike for so long? Don't your legs get tired? Our wings are to us what your legs are to you. They take us where we need to go.

Most of the team doesn't look like us at all. In fact, most of them can't even fly! However, everyone brings a different perspective and value to the team, even if it's not apparent at first. We also realized that each member of the team is a leader regardless of whether they have a title that refers to leadership. Most of us are confident, procrastinate, make decisions, set goals, face conflict, are challenged with communication, and are looking to find peace at some point in our lives.

Are you familiar with the phrase, "If you want something done right, do it yourself?" Ann's dad, a workaholic, championed this way of thinking. He shared it with her throughout her childhood and teen years, while she worked beside him in his business. It became part of her mantra. Don't get me wrong, I am not by any means criticizing her dad—his generation subscribed to this way of thinking, and he taught her so many things for which she is grateful. Much of her business sense comes from him. It's just that together we can achieve so much more. In the end, does it matter how we get there as long as we get where we're going? Today, just about everyone works in teams. There's plenty of room for all of us to be successful if we come from a place of abundance and rely on each other's strengths as well as our own.

Like the introduction shares, we have a variety of "team members" within ourselves and those in the workplace with similar traits. If you can lead your team within, you can lead and support the team on the outside that may be challenged with the same things you are or have been challenged with in the past. You'll be able to identify with each team member you meet in this book and gain insight on how they can each support you in achieving your goals and being the best version of yourself you can be.

Have I piqued your interest yet? Are you wondering where I'm going with this and what you can learn about leadership from my team and me and how you can embrace it?

Good!

We, the geese, in our own kind of way, knew about working and living together, total quality management, and about taking turns leading long before Deming introduced his fourteen points to the world. We know each team member adds value and has something to offer. Each one of us knows when to lead, when to follow, and when to stay behind and help the one who has fallen and needs time to regroup or heal. We have learned to ask for and extend help to support each other.

When our lead goose is tired and needs a break, it takes a different place in the formation, and another goose takes the lead. If one needs to take a break and rest, at least one other stays behind with him. How awesome would it feel to know you have people who can share in leading a project, take your place in line even if only for a while, or hang out with you while you take a break? Each one of our team members knows they have a role to play and value to bring to the team, even if the value some of our members bring isn't obvious at first. If all of us are given the chance to learn and lead, we can expand our knowledge base and be even more prepared to step in the next time. We get it. People take pride in what they do and have a hard time letting go and letting others take the lead. Ann used to think she had to have all the answers when she was in a leadership position. Not because she was cocky or anything like that, but because if she had the responsibility, she didn't want to let anyone down. A leader was supposed to have the answers, right?

Heck, no. Wise and effective leaders understand that they don't need to know all the answers, they need to know where to find the answers and how to ask the right questions. In our experience, we need to surround ourselves with team members who are smarter than we are and know how to leverage our own and each other's strengths. When we surround ourselves with friends, the challenges are less lonely, and the joys and successes are more fun to celebrate.

There really is a leader in every seat. You don't have to be in a leadership position to position yourself as a leader. Most people take pride in their work. The funny thing about pride is that it can be both a blessing and a curse. Some say pride is a personal commitment which separates excellence from mediocrity. That's the blessing. It can also be a curse because it can stop us from asking for support when we need it. Yep, it goes back to thinking we have to do it on our own because if we asked for help, it would show weakness. We believe the healthy ones ask for help.

It's a balancing act, knowing when to lead, when to follow, when to stay behind, and when to move forward. Like I shared earlier, if one of our team needs a break, two of us stay with the team member until it is ready and able to fly and rejoin the team and resume the journey or leave for whatever reason. What happens when you need a break and how can you feel comfortable asking for what you need? Share leadership. It can work in many situations. Just like each of your inner team members brings value to your team.

It's a journey to learn how to capitalize on your strengths, what type of leader you want to be and, of equal importance, the type you don't want to be. I bet you can think of people you want to emulate and others you don't. You may think, "but I enjoy being independent!" So does Ann. She used to think she could do everything on her own. Growing up, she had goals, and she wanted to learn what it took to accomplish them, then to be left alone to accomplish them. We all can do things on our own. Yet can you achieve the best result on your own? It may depend what you're working on at the moment.

Asking for help is still difficult for Ann. Years ago, it was not even part of her vocabulary; however, it is now. She grew up watching a lot of successful people. They all looked like they had it all together and under control all the time. It looked as if they did it on their own. They didn't. Behind and around successful people is a village who has supported them in one way or another. Most successful people know the importance of helping others achieve their goals, too. It's give and take. We believe it's a balance of being self-sufficient and relying on other people—you know the village and the saying, "it takes a village..." It does take a village. Each one of us plays an important role in whatever village we are a part of. Your relationships are like geese flying in formation. There is safety and knowledge in numbers. It's like synergy—the outcome is greater than the sum of all parts. You're going to meet our village in this book.

Simon Sinek, an author and perhaps known most for his TED talk focused on the concept of "Why," suggests that leaders not only learn to listen but also learn to speak last. I totally agree with him. Ann used to think as a leader and parent she had to have the answers and tell people what the solutions were. This way, she would earn respect and demonstrate she knew what she was doing. When in reality, it takes a team and all the ideas and skills each person offers. Is it a good idea as a leader to share our ideas? Absolutely. The challenge is that many times the leader shares their idea first and their team thinks what's the use—our leader already has his or her mind made up. So, ask questions, listen to your team's ideas, share your thoughts, and work together on the solution. I know. It can be a dance.

What do you do when your team members show up and want to lead? Let them have the opportunity to lead whether it be a meeting, a conversation, or a project. Remember how you learned? Somebody gave you the chance to lead. Help them if they need it. Partner with them. Let them know it's okay to try new strategies. If they work great! If not, learn and move on. Just like the members of our team, they will show up and remain with us for as long as they are needed at home and in the workplace.

How do you know when it's time to stop and change direction? This is hard because, are we stopping because it's hard or because we really don't want or can't do this anymore? Stopping for a break can refresh our perspective. Ann paused, pondered, pivoted, and proceeded when deciding finally to write this book. And it was hard to admit the first draft needed to be revamped. However, the good news is, you get to meet my friends and me.

The sky's the limit for our teams to imagine what could be. Fresh air and new ideas! Granted, we fly south each year, but we don't always have to take the same path. There's plenty of room for everyone to be successful if you come from a place of abundance and rely on each other's strengths as well as your own. How many times do you think you have to take a specific path when in reality, it is like the broad endless blue sky? What if you could be open to another's path in getting you or the team to the same place? How freeing it could be to have partners to share the responsibilities and the celebration.

When the elephant, the squirrel, the rabbit, and the rest of the team take turns leading, following, and collaborating we all win. We all grow. So how do you know when to lead, when to follow and when to listen to the inner and outer team? Sometimes it's clear. Sometimes it's not. For us, we work to determine who has the right skills for each situation. By the way, it's also important to remember that you can develop and strengthen the skills you need. When you give someone or take the opportunity someone gives you, everyone can grow and develop into the leader and person they want to become. You're going to want to be promoted or retire someday and it's a good idea to support people in their development because they will be in charge when you've moved on, gotten promoted, or retired!

Ann and the Transitional Management Team: Leading, Letting Others Lead, and Collaboration

Late in the '90s, when Ann worked for the American Cancer Society, the National Organization reorganized their entire structure. They moved from over fifty divisions to seventeen divisions. What a shakeup in the organization and leadership roles! Minnesota, Wisconsin, South Dakota, and Iowa were merging into one division, known as the Midwest Division. Ann and five of her Colleagues from three of the states were asked to serve on the Transitional Management Team with four of the senior leaders. They were Design Team Leaders and Facilitators. The role of the Design Teams—to recommend which projects the new Division would keep and which ones would be eliminated as well as a potential structure for each of the six areas. The Transitional Management Team's major role and responsibility was to evaluate the recommendations from the Design Teams and determine how to proceed in structuring the new division.

One day, Ann shared with Jari (the Executive Vice President), her supervisor at the time, that she was struggling because she didn't know if she was doing a very good job leading the team. Ann shared that she didn't have the answers to all the questions asked during the many difficult conversations held by her team. The team, challenged in discovering the answers, had a multitude of lively conversations. She felt as if she was letting Jari down and wondered if they made the right choice in asking her to lead the Programming Design Team.

Jari, taking advantage of this learning opportunity, simply stated, "You weren't chosen because you had all the answers. We chose you because you are an excellent facilitator. You involve everyone in conversations and ensure that all voices are heard."

Ann's parents raised her to be independent. She used to think she had to have all the answers. After all, that's what leaders, parents, and independent people do. Right? Not even close to being a yes. She was so very wrong. She learned through experiences like her divorce, leading teams, and becoming a mom—the healthy ones get help.

On that day, in that moment, Ann realized a valuable lesson: a leader doesn't have to have all the answers—they need to work with their team and help them discover the solutions. As a facilitator, she learned the value of giving others the chance to lead the conversations, jumping back in if the conversation went awry. Leading, following, and collaborating all work together.

Ann and ICF Iowa: Speaking Last

When Ann served as President of the ICF Iowa Chapter, it was her intent to bring the issues needed to be discussed to the Board and ask the Board members what they thought. It was so challenging to speak last, not because she didn't want to hear what everyone had to say, but because she didn't want anyone to think she didn't have an opinion or answer. She worked hard to remember that she did not want to come across as if she had made up her mind on what she thought they should do, because many times she hadn't. Every once in a while, she had a strong opinion and shared it. However, in the end, it was always a board decision. The good news, like the geese, the team was successful because they collaborated and collectively made the best decision for the chapter, not for one person. John Maxwell stated at a conference she attended, "If you're the smartest person in the room, you're in the wrong room." She was blessed in being in the right room with the board because that "flock of geese" on the board had amazing wisdom, a plethora of ideas, and took turns taking the lead based on their main strength. They were successful not because of one, but because of many.

Noah and His Grandma: Leading Each Other

When Noah was entering sixth grade, his grandma, Ann's mom, came to stay with him for ten days while Doug and Ann were traveling to Rome with their church. It was the only vacation taken without him when he was growing up. Of course, when they shared with him that his grandma was coming to stay with him, he asked, "Why?" and then stated, "I'm perfectly capable of taking care of myself." He shared he would only use the microwave and not the oven, and he would set an alarm each night so he would get up and be on time for school.

As a twelve-year-old, he didn't understand that leaving a child his age on his own for ten days would, without a doubt, land them in jail for quite some time.

His grandma did a great job of taking care of him. Though she shared, she felt at times it was the opposite—he took care of her. During her visit, though she took the lead in cooking and maintaining the schedule, Noah had the opportunity to take the lead in ordering pictures when picture day occurred during her stay. Grandma had no idea what to order when Noah showed her the picture packet, which needed to be returned before his parents came home. His response to her sharing that she did not know what pictures to order—"No worries, Grandma. I know what Mom orders."

He sat down. He marked what package to order. He then went downstairs, opened the safe and took out cash to send with the order. What a proud moment for a sixth-grader to take the lead in ordering his own pictures. Upon returning home and opening the picture packet, Ann observed a handsome kid with chaotic hair. In her head the initial response was—"Hmmm, we may have to have retakes." In a split second, she replaced her initial response with marveling at the wonderful image captured of their independent, proud, son. She refrained from speaking a word that would have crushed his confidence and spirit. To this day, that picture is one of her favorites because it represents a boy taking the lead when the opportunity presented itself. Just like the geese, the one with the strength takes the lead and then turns it over to the next one to lead.

Aree's story: Similar and Yet So Different - Everyone Brings Value to the Team

Aree and Ann met in Mitch Matthew's Acceleration Mastermind. They worked together virtually for over a year, then finally met in person during a weekend workshop in Des Moines. It's funny how it can take months and sometimes years to grow a relationship with some people and others you can feel perfectly at ease with almost immediately. Aree is one of those people who Ann felt an instant connection with. Aree has a knack for making people feel comfortable and part of the team. Collaboration is one of her strengths. She works with people to help them work better with their peers and teams.

While coaching a rather large team, which was working on an important and very visible national project, she realized that while all team members had similar backgrounds, skills, job titles, and education, they all had different ideas and communication styles which got in their way. The company had done a good job of assembling the team with members who had different strengths; the challenge—each had a different way of communicating and relating to one another.

In working with DiSC and the Personal Coaching Styles Inventory, Ann completely understood where Aree was coming from. Some team members were interested in research, others in relationships, and others more focused on achieving the goal more quickly than the rest. Some liked to lead, others followed, and yet all learned that each one had something to add to the team and their overall success. Aree worked with the team and helped them understand each other's styles and what was most important to the other and what each needed to move forward. During their conversation, they both agreed it's about valuing what each person brings to the team and letting that strength shine through. Ann shared with Aree that during her team coaching certification training, two of the most important questions to ask a team are, "What is your purpose and what is it that your team can do that no other team can bring to the organization?"

Aree had a conversation with the team and shared what the different styles wanted and how each could adapt their style to work more efficiently with the others. It did not mean they changed who they were—as each brought value to the team; it was all about adapting and flexing their style.

The outcome: all were better able to communicate and reduce conflict between each other. They even had a successful product rollout.

We included Aree's strategies in the strategy section of this chapter and on the next page.

1. Make no assumptions—even if members have similar backgrounds.

2. Look at things as a team—what do we need to do to achieve the greater good while still staying true to who we are?

3. Move people around and let them use their strengths on each project.

4. It's okay to let different people lead: Successful leaders don't have to always be in the lead role—besides that's how leaders learn and develop. This was an AHA moment for the leader of the team.

Lessons Learned

- Team = We/Me

- You don't have to have all the answers: Successful leaders know their strengths and when to ask for help.

- All team members bring value to the team and are of equal importance; they just have different responsibilities.

- There is productivity in working together. When you have a common goal or purpose, it's easier to collaborate because you're all working toward the same thing. That noise you hear is our team in constant communication with each other.

- Communicate often.

- Communication is challenging.

- Communication is important. Geese talk to each other in their own language and seem to always understand one another. Humans are not always so lucky. You can speak the same language, use the same words, and still not understand what the other person is saying.

How many times have you interpreted the words spoken and the tone in which they were spoken in an incorrect manner? Did you assume what was meant based on your own preconceived notions? How many times have we asked clarifying questions? Or asked any question at all? We all have our own perceptions about how we understand what people are saying. Your perception is your reality, even if it's not true. Asking questions with kindness and compassion can aid us in truly understanding the other person.

- Communicate until you get it right.

- When you face obstacles, you can choose to keep going or stop. Usually, the most challenging times are those when you learn and grow the most. Ann says this a lot, but it's so true and honestly, she has to remind herself of this or she'd go crazy and would have quit many times when things got tough. Life isn't easy, but it's possible and there's so much to celebrate.

- Support and help one another—there will come a time when you need help, too.

- It's okay to take a break and regroup. There will come a day when you will be the support system to another person. It is reassuring to know you don't have to go it alone, and it's perfectly okay to ask for help and to let the person whose strength you need know when you need help.

- As a life, leadership, and team coach, Ann knows her clients have the answers—they just don't always know it yet. Parents come to understand, with patience, that their kiddos can figure out the answers if given time and support. When they discover the solution on their own and use their critical thinking skills, they own the process and the outcome.

- Ask tough questions with kindness and compassion. Then wait patiently, quietly, and really listen for the response.
- Teams need everyone.
- Ask for help even when it's hard.
- Give people the opportunity to lead and follow.
- You don't always have to be in the lead to be the leader.
- Each team member within has a purpose and role to plan in our success.
- Stick together—there is strength and wisdom in numbers.
- There is no "I" in the word "team," but there is a "we"—just turn the "me" upside down! Is there also a "me" in team? Yes, it's the part you contribute to the team. Enjoy being part of something that's bigger than yourself.
- Together we really can achieve more.
- It's more fun when we share our success and challenges with others.
- Just as teams have people who bring different strengths to the team, our team members have strengths and limitations or weaknesses. Weaknesses are strengths that have not yet been developed. You have the ability and the choice to choose which strengths you develop.
- It helps to have a common goal.
- Encourage and support each other.
- Make no assumptions — even if members have similar backgrounds.
- Rely on each other's strengths, as well as your own.

- Successful leaders don't have to always be in the lead role—besides that's how leaders learn and develop.
- We are usually most successful when we know when to lead, when to follow, and when we all work together, we *will* accomplish the goal.

My Strengths

- Provide opportunities to and encourage others to lead.
- Collaborate with all team members.
- Have the courage to lead and let go.
- Camaraderie.
- Ability to listen to everyone.
- Recognizing our strengths and the strengths of others.

Your Strengths (List the strengths you see in yourself when it comes to leading, following, and collaborating.)

Strategies: Choose the one(s) which will best serve you.

- Share the vision with the team.
- Listen to each other and learn to speak last.
- Decide on your mindset. How do you feel? How do you want to feel? How do you want others to feel?
- Communicate. Communicate. Communicate.
- Find people you trust by getting to know them.
- Be trustworthy.
- Take turns leading: Provide others with the opportunity to lead.

- Pause, Ponder, Pivot, Proceed.
  - Pause — think about the situation. We may pause for a cause or of equal importance have cause to pause.
  - Ponder the situation and where you're going:
    - Ask your team and yourself some questions including but not limited to:
      - What is our purpose?
      - Is this goal still important to the team or me?
      - Are we or am I heading in the right direction based upon our goals and what we said is important?
      - Do I/we have the right people in the right places or positions?
      - Do I/we have the resources we need?
    - Pivot — change directions if the situation warrants.
    - Proceed — keep moving in the direction of your goal(s).
- Look at things as a team — What do we need to do to achieve the greater good while still staying true to who we are?
- Let others lead.

Your Reflection

Reflection Questions: Answer here or in a separate journal.

1. What do I enjoy about leading?
2. When am I confident and comfortable letting go and letting others lead?
3. When is collaboration exhilarating? When is it draining or depleting?

Your Biggest Takeaway(s) Regarding Leading, Following, and Collaborating

Your Action Plan

Here is an example of what your action plan may look like. Remember it's your plan not mine, this is only an example to support you in getting started. Choose the action which will support you in moving forward. There is space for you to write your personal plan of action at the end of the example.

1. *Goal: Let others lead*
2. *Action: Next time there is an opportunity to share facilitation of a meeting or lead a project, I will make a conscious effort to let someone else lead.*
3. *Who will support me? My supervisor and co-workers*
4. *Date: Next meeting/project*
5. *How will I know I'm making progress? I won't be leading the project or meeting. I will be there to support the person leading.*

Your Turn: Answer here or in a separate journal.

1. Goal:

2. Action:

3. Who can support you?

4. Date to begin:

5. How will you know you made progress?

I'm excited and looking forward to introducing you to the members of my team and sharing with you what was learned when we met the squirrel, the elephant, the rabbit, and some of their friends. So, let's meet the team within, discover what they have to offer, and how each can support you, as well as have some fun! Oh, and by the way, you don't have to read the chapters in order. If one of my team members and what they have to share resonates with you based on where you are right now, read that one first.

Additional Resources

- *Think Again* by Adam Grant.

- *Uncommon Leaders* by Ruchira Chaudhary.

- YouTube video — https://www.youtube.com/watch?v=urrYhnaKvy4&t=330s (How to Be a Leader) TED Talk by Simon Sinek. In this video Sinek has many excellent tips about what it takes to be a leader. One of the most significant tips is this: he shares that there are plenty of people who are willing and want to help you. You just need to ask. They don't jump in because they don't know you need or want help. The geese and Ann believe knowing when to ask for help can be one of your greatest strengths. It also takes courage to ask for help.

- YouTube video — https://www.youtube.com/watch?v=Ek2fkneLcjM (Teamwork — Lessons from the Geese — The Art of Teamwork (2 min)) This short video shares a valuable lesson we can learn about teamwork from the geese. They demonstrate when to lead and when to follow each other. Through collaboration they arrive at their intended destination.

The Butterfly

Change and Transformation

"When you're through changing...you're through."

Bruce Barton

To change or not to change. That is the question. Sometimes you get to decide whether or not you change something. Other times, the choice is made for you. When you don't have a choice in the change, it may feel as if something is happening that you don't want.

Ever wonder why people cringe when they hear the word *change*? Do you cringe when you think about a large change in your life? Or does the thought of something changing excite you? It might depend on what the change is and whether you had anything to do with the decision behind the change. Like it or not, the bottom line is that sometimes you have a choice and sometimes you don't. Ann's friend Sinikka says that change is a process, not an event. I think she's right. One thing is certain about change—it's inevitable. So how can you embrace it, figure out how to best work through it, and even grow from it? Because let's face it, to get through it, you have to go through it. We all do!

I love change, and when there's a change on the horizon, the geese let me lead. After all, there are few animals that know more about change than the butterfly! I can support you in working through change regardless of whether it's wanted or what the change itself is. Even when change is a choice, like marriage, moving to a new city, buying a house, starting a new job or career, or something else you are looking forward to, it can still bc challenging. Sometimes it feels as if it takes forever for things to change and other times it happens faster than the speed of light. Both ways can be scary!

I think it's all in the way you look at change and approach it. Usually, one of the first questions people have is related to the world's most famous radio station *WII.FM—"What's in it for me?"*

When a change happens, most want to know how the change is going to affect things such as lifestyle, job, responsibilities, workload, and salary. The list goes on and on. The question becomes, how can you lead yourself and others through change? Ann's husband shared with her that when people hear the word change, they subconsciously drop the *Ch* and add an *R* at the end—transforming *change* to *anger*. Anger, many times, shows up when you don't feel as if you have a choice. Even when you make the choice to change something, it doesn't mean it's not without challenges.

Change can transform you, your peers, or your organization into something even more stunning than where you are now. It can be a physical, emotional, or spiritual transformation. There are all kinds of ways change takes place. Many times, the changes that are the most difficult are the ones on which we don't decide. It doesn't mean you're opposed to them; it just means somebody else made the decision and you are going to have to figure out how to work and lead yourself, and many times others, through the change.

How do you feel when a change is coming? You may think it depends on whether you had a say in not only the change, but how the change will occur. If someone shared that by making the change a positive transformation or outcome would take place, what feelings would that invoke? I notice when people hear the word *change* they groan, and when they hear the word *transformation* they usually have a positive feeling or outlook on the situation. Transformation feels positive, like something will make an impact and an everlasting effect on the world. Yet, in order to make a transformation, a change still needs to be made. You can't get away from it no matter how hard you try. When I lead you through change, it's not about me—it's about you and how it will affect you, your team members, and maybe the world. Make sure to keep that in mind!

Spring is my favorite season. It's seen as a time for growth, new beginnings, new life, and hope. While change happens in all seasons of life, this is the time people can see the change and transformation in me. As the butterfly on your team, this is my time to lead. It is part of my job to remind you of the beauty of change. However, I didn't start out in my current state. I am reminded of the sacrifices and changes needed for me to get here.

The caterpillar had to spin a cocoon and give up his current state for me to come into being. This isn't explicitly stating that you need to give up everything. In fact, your values, knowledge, and experience will serve you greatly as you go through the many changes in your life. But it does mean that the caterpillar leaves behind what he knows and was comfortable with, and instead allows himself to experience an incredible transformation in order for me to emerge into a beautiful, transformed state: a butterfly with wings.

I am grateful for the change. Change can be good, like the caterpillar which allows itself to work to complete its commitment to emerge the version of itself it always knew it could and longed to be. Is there a change or transformation toward which you are working by your choice or someone else's? You don't have to change for the sake of change. Make the change that makes sense. Or if the change is happening to you, decide if you can live with it or if a fresh change needs to occur: a job, a move?

What is it about change that is challenging and painful for you as well as others? The changes I see people struggle with and worry about the most are the ones over which they have little or no control. They don't have a clear vision of what's on the other side of the change, nor has anyone informed them of the vision or the reason (the why) for the change. Do some of the following questions sound familiar when you and your peers or friends are going through change?

- Why do we have to change course?
- Aren't things okay the way they are?
- How will the change affect me?
- How will it affect my family?
- How will it affect my income?
- How will it affect my lifestyle?
- Will I still have a job?
- Will there be changes in my responsibilities?
- Will I have to learn an entirely new system?
- Why does technology change so often?
- Will my hours change?
- What will my new job be like?
- If I move, will I make friends?
- Will I like the new city?
- Do I have the knowledge and skills to do the job?

- What will my purpose be if I retire?
- What is it about change that is so challenging and painful?

The list goes on and on.

How does this relate to yourself and others when leading your team within, leadership, and change?

You get to choose how you react or respond to change. You can concentrate on only the caterpillar, what is now, the challenges you face, and what you are giving up, or you can focus on how to manage and overcome the challenges or obstacles and what possibilities the change may bring. I think it's perfectly okay to grieve the loss. With change, even the good ones, there is still loss. When Noah left for college, Ann grieved the loss of seeing him daily. Don't get me wrong; she embraced the change and the transformation to come, and she *still* grieved.

It helps Ann to remember that grief and loss are part of transformation. Knowing they most likely aren't going to last forever is comforting. Focusing on the outcome or end result, supports Ann in getting through not only Noah moving but continues to support her in navigating the many changes life brings. She takes great solace in knowing Noah is transforming into the man he wants to be. Each change in her life, both the ones she chose, and others chosen for her, have, in the end, turned out the way they were supposed to. They provided her with valuable insight, which continues to guide her in becoming the best version of herself she can be.

Sometimes, to get through it, you have to go through it.

My superpower is to encourage you to spread your wings as well as encourage others to spread their wings. Keep your eyes on the end goal. Stress happens when you take your eyes off the goal and focus on only the obstacles. Don't get me wrong, you'll want to identify, acknowledge, and plan how to address and overcome the obstacles. It's also important to focus on the potential end results.

I remember a student in one of Ann's classes asking a question. I don't know what the question was, and it doesn't really matter. Ann made the comment that she felt like Ziggy in one of his comic strips, when he said, "Just when I learned all the answers, they changed all the questions."

Change can be like this. Just when you feel the change is complete, something else changes.

As humans, you may find yourselves moving from caterpillars to butterflies and back to caterpillars. Transforming into butterflies during many stages of your life is natural. You learn, grow, move toward your goals, and accomplish them personally or professionally only to find yourselves caterpillars again wrapped in a new cocoon of learning to once again emerge from a cocoon even more beautiful, more confident and successful than the last. Strong, graceful, and fragile at the same time.

Ann Moves to Florida at Nineteen

As a little girl, Ann always wondered what would happen if she picked up and moved to somewhere different than her hometown in the Midwest. Florida—that's it—she visited it several times on vacation, so she thought when she grew up, *I'm moving to Florida.* After graduating from a one-year business college, she and Renee, a "friend" (or so she thought at the time), whom she met at school, decided to move to Florida. Hope, optimism about the future and the possibilities that lie ahead, constantly occupied her thoughts. Her dream was becoming a reality.

She could not wait!

I'm certain Ann's parents wondered; *Will she be safe? Will she find a job? Will she make excellent decisions?* The "will she" questions went on and on.

No job. No clue. Just a desire for a new adventure which included looking forward to an apartment of her own, a career she would love, and hopefully meeting a boyfriend. It was going to be great!

Let the adventure begin.

Yeah, I'm guessing you have an idea of how this worked out or didn't.

Ann knew no one in Florida except her "friend" who had agreed to move with her. They planned on living with Renee's friends.

Honestly, just about everything that could go wrong—did. I'll share the short version of what happened today. Maybe you'll get a chance to hear the dirty details in-depth some other time!

For now, let's focus on the hardest-hitting moments...

The first red flag should have been when Ann arrived at Renee's house after attending a party, the night before they were to move, only to have Renee ask Ann what she would do if she (the friend) decided not to move to Florida. You do not want to know what Ann's 19-year-old mind wanted to say. She politely mustered up all the strength she had, and simply replied, "I've turned down jobs to make this move and I hope you still decide to come with me. But I'm leaving at 7:00 a.m. with or without you. I hope your friends will let me stay with them until I find a job because I don't know anyone in Florida." She then turned and went to bed.

At 7:00 a.m. the next morning, they left. Each was in her own car, ready for an adventure. Everything Ann owned had been crammed into her little red Chevy. Renee's car followed behind.

After staying with Renee's friends for a month, they rented a duplex and secured jobs.

The second red flag came when, within three weeks of moving into their own place, Renee's boyfriend moved to Florida and into their duplex.

The third red flag flew when, after another three weeks, Renee and the boyfriend announced they were moving back to St. Louis. They asked Ann what she was going to do. Ann shared that she was staying. She called her parents, in tears, multiple times from a payphone as this was before cell phones and before she had a landline. To this day Ann doesn't know how much money they spent on phone calls. Thank goodness her generous and supportive parents let her call collect! Talk about feeling alone! Thankfully, her parents offered to help her until she found a job, a place to live and rode out this one of many bumps in the road of life.

Renee and her boyfriend left. They lost their deposit. Ann moved out and into a motel on her own for a few weeks. She found two roommates. She enjoyed her job as an assistant manager in a little sunglass place. She loved the beach. She relished her independence. She thought life was good.

The fourth red flag arrived several months later. Ann and Patti, her roommate, the nice one, discovered the other roommate, who had the apartment, was charging them rent where they were paying for everything, and she paid for nothing. I won't go into what Ann and Patti thought of her.

In the meantime, one of Ann's sisters moved to Florida (which was a good thing). They all moved into Patti's parent's house in Florida. I should share that Patti's brother and four of his friends moved into the house at about the same time.

Patti dated a guy named Carl. Ann's sister dated Patti's brother. Each couple had their own room. The other "boys" shared the living room. Mustering up all the courage she could find, Ann just looked at the "boys" and matter-of-factly stated, "Don't talk to me. Don't touch me. Don't bother me." Then she claimed the den next to the living room as her space. Talk about a full house. Talk about organized chaos! Talk about unwanted change. What a disaster.

Red flag number five arrived when at work, Ann had just gotten passed over as manager of the little sunglass place because she was too young. Forget she did the job for a few months just after her manager resigned.

On Easter Sunday, after three weeks of working with no days off, she hung out at the beach with the boys, Patti, and her sister. After a few beers (19 was the legal age at the time) she looked around and thought, "This is not what I envisioned my life to look like here. I'm anything but happy. Yet, if I move back, people will think I'm a failure." Overwhelmed with emotion, failure or not, Ann made a decision to leave Florida. Soon.

Ann gave her two-week notice the very next day. She headed back to Illinois on a Saturday night and drove as far as she could, all her belongings crammed into her little red Chevy—but this time they included a little black and white cat. She and the cat got a motel room. The next day she drove another fourteen hours, got a hotel room, and finished the last six hours the next day, arriving back in Illinois at her parent's house midday. That's where she stayed for the summer. During that time, she painted the entire inside of their house and picked herself up off the ground determined to make the most out of the situation.

Knowing her strength and confidence were shattered, Ann's parents assured her all would work out. Start over, only this time with more experience. They were right.

Digging deep and relying on her determination, perseverance, and willingness to embrace yet another change, she found a manager trainee job at a fabric store in Davenport, Iowa in the fall. She still can't believe Bob hired her, because when he asked her where she saw herself in five years, she told him she wanted his job. Believe me, Ann wasn't and isn't usually that direct. But the changes that she had gone through and obstacles she overcame, had given her the courage to be open in sharing her goals. Ann stayed with the company for six years until a major reorganization took place. That's a whole different story.

Little did she know at the time, she had far from failed. She succeeded because she took a chance. She followed a dream. It didn't work out. It took her years to realize the true transformation happened within and would serve her well when in the future it was time for another change, one that she had control over. Even though the future was unknown, she would be ready and have the courage to make the change.

Ann was grateful for having learned it was okay to take a different path, and that you can and will make it through obstacles of change no matter who decides there will be a change. At the time, moving back home seemed like a major challenge. It was one of the most challenging decisions regarding change she had faced at that point in her life. Once in a leadership position, Ann thought that having a career and making decisions that affected hundreds, perhaps thousands, of people a day was challenging and quite stressful. Little did she know it was only preparing her, as many changes do, for her most important, not to mention the most challenging and certainly most rewarding "career," she would have: that of being a mom.

Bottom line—her life didn't turn out the way she expected when she moved to Florida. Does she have regrets about the decision to move to Florida? Absolutely not! No regrets. To this day she doesn't play the "What If?" game. She moved. It didn't work out. Something better worked out. If she had not had the courage to make a change and move to Florida, she may wonder what would have happened if she hadn't moved. She doesn't wonder that at all.

Through it all, a butterfly emerged. She had to break out of the cocoon and stand on her own two feet. I know she didn't feel like one of those beautiful butterflies, but she flew all the same. Thank goodness Ann's parents encouraged her to spread her wings.

It is said you will regret more what you didn't do rather than the things you did. Besides, she has some marvelous stories to share around the fire, over a cup of tea or a glass of wine.

We have roots and wings—both of which are necessary.

Noah Shares His Dream of Moving After College

Her son made it clear that he wanted to attend a four-year college and then move somewhere other than Iowa, because he'd lived in Iowa his entire life. Why would he stay there in the cold when there's an entire world to explore and a new adventure awaited?

With confidence, and some sadness as any mom would have but didn't let it show, she said, "Go for it. We have your back."

The up and downside? He is so like her.

On the inside a plethora of emotion flowed through her mind and body. Will he be safe? Will he be happy? Will he find his way? How do I help him with the transition to living on his own even if in a college dorm? What transformation will take place? She thought, "Oh my gosh, I've turned into my mother!"

Ann remembered how, when she announced she was moving to Florida, her parents were supportive and asked her a variety of questions similar to the ones above. Never "questioning" the decision, just asking questions for clarification, as much for her to be certain of her decision as for them. Her parents were a wealth of information and most importantly a safe place to fall while going through each change and transformation the Florida experience offered.

Did she miss her son when he moved? Absolutely! Was she thrilled he wanted to move out and go to college? Absolutely! Like her parents did for her, she wanted to do for her son. She knew it was her and her husband's responsibility to help him grow and become the best version of himself he could be. Eighteen years of slowly and meticulously working his way out of the "cocoon" to be on his own and continue developing into that beautiful butterfly was always the goal. Time to venture out into the world, spread his wings, find his way, and achieve his goals. When his caterpillar shows up and he wants to learn a new skill, or if he gets stuck in that cocoon as he works on yet another transformation, Ann and Doug will be there to encourage him to keep working his way to the next transformation, which will be securing a full-time job—hopefully one he will enjoy!

While he may be a little nervous (if he wasn't Ann would really be concerned), wondering what life will bring and if he will find a job, he has the strength and confidence to try. Partly because he has tried a variety of things throughout his life and experienced success, as well as trials and tribulations. He also knows he has his parent's support to spread his wings.

Switching Majors

As adults, you always want what is best for your children. Truth be told, you want them to have a better life than you had, no matter how great your life is. You always want things to be better for them. I am reminded of the time Noah embarked on his college journey.

He began as a typical college freshman, full of excitement and independence, he enrolled in the college of business. He switched to a different college within the same university. He wanted to take a different path than when he began. Two and a half years into his journey, he wasn't certain if he had made the right decision. He questioned himself, admitted he didn't see the value of the first path, and now wondered if he should have stayed the course. You can't change the past, but you can learn from it. He could go back, take some classes, and change majors. On the other hand, was there a different path, which could lead him to the goal he wanted to achieve?

His goal at the time was to land a good job that he enjoyed, earn a comfortable living, and make a difference in the world. His transformation from being anxious and stuck to being "unstuck" as a more confident and excited young man was amazing. After hours of asking him questions, not all at the same time—though Ann is the Queen Mom of the Spanish Inquisition, giving him space to think, and really listening to what he said and didn't say, he decided to finish the double major and minor which he was so close to earning.

His next step was to apply to graduate school and pursue a master's degree, with two tracks, one in Business Analytics and one in Finance. These degrees would open doors and provide the opportunities for which he was looking. Like the caterpillar continues to learn, he grows, he changes and continues transforming into the person he wants to be. He was accepted to grad school and at the time of writing this book was working on his degree.

Lessons Learned

- Change is inevitable. Change is uncomfortable. Change takes time. Change is hard; even the changes you know will be beneficial in helping you get what you want, like marriage, moving, or changing jobs. Change takes work. You can change your course, you can change it back, and you can change to a different course to achieve your goal. Change can bring about the transformation for which you've been waiting.

- If you concentrate on only the caterpillar and what is currently comfortable, you might miss the future possibility the change will bring. He snuggles into his cocoon over the winter and transforms into a beautiful creature taking its place in the circle of life, grounded in his pursuit of what he is to become, knowing for him it will take an entire season to transform.

- Many times, situations start out messy and then turn into beautiful works of art. This book started out messy! Ideas splashing like gigantic waves against a reef, rolling around in Ann's head. Doug walked into her office, looked at the sea of colored post-it notes stuck to the hutch on her desk, and asked what those were. She simply looked at him and stated, "That is my brain and a book on post-it notes." They both laughed, not because it wasn't true but just at the chaos of notes. The good news, it wasn't all in her head anymore and she didn't have to remember all of those thoughts because they were in fact on post-it notes. She did, however, need to go back and sort the ideas into books, chapters, and mind-maps.

- You can embrace and manage change, or you can let it manage you. You decide what version of yourself you want to be when experiencing change. You have the ability to transform your thoughts, the way you interact with people, and your actions to become the person you want to be and in choosing how you will handle change.

- You can drop the *Ch* and add the *R* and feel *anger* **or** you can remain open to the beauty of the transformation and what change can bring on the other side.

- There's an old saying that says, "In the end, it all works out. If it hasn't worked out, it's not the end." I think that's true. And of course, once things have worked out, usually another change begins. You, as well as your team members, with grace and patience can and will change as you grow and learn through all the experiences in life.

- Allow yourself to be open to change, try new things, seek new possibilities, make mistakes, get up and continue learning and succeeding. When you give yourself the grace to continue growing and embrace change, you can also give others that same grace to try, fail, succeed, learn, grow, transform, celebrate change, and become the person they want to be.

- Keep the values you hold dear as you navigate the change.

- Ann's good friends from the Jaycees, an organization focused on teaching people between the ages of 18–39 to be effective leaders through community service, used to say, "if you're not growin, you're dying."

- Blooming, reinventing ourselves, and growing are part of our journey. Let's grow together as we stretch our imagination and our talents and continue developing into the people we want to be. You have to be in the game if you're going to play the game or if you want to change the rules.

- Everyone is a work in progress. Some caterpillars are beautiful. Some, not so much, but no matter how or where they begin, they have the potential to turn into something beautiful that can spread their wings and fly.

- There have been plenty of movies about the butterfly effect. This is a concept that explains how one incident, one change, one person affects another person's life. Sometimes you know how you affect another and many times, more often than not, you may never know the effect you have on others.

- If the caterpillar focused on only the obstacles, he may give up before he made the transformation. He knows it's going to be hard yet keeps on going.

- You can change the direction and course on which you have embarked. Get in the game. Do something. If it doesn't turn out the way you want, change directions. Think about what all of us can accomplish if we are willing to work for it.

My Strengths

- Knowing change can bring about beautiful transformations and lead you through change no matter who decides the change.

- I give you the opportunity to grow.

- Determination to get through the change to the transformation.

Your Strengths (List the strengths you see in yourself when it comes to navigating change.)

Strategies: Choose the one(s) which will best serve you.

- Decide how you are going to handle the change.

- Give yourself permission to laugh, cry, be angry, sad, and feel what you need to, so you can work through the emotions to positively move yourself forward.

- Ask questions. When change occurs, the person making the change usually shares or considers the following. It is information people want to know when a change is going to happen, scheduled or not. People want answers to or will ask the "W" questions when a change is on the horizon:

  ○ **Who** is involved and who benefits from the change?

  ○ **What** change or transformation is needed and how does it benefit the company, clients, and team members?

  ○ **When** is the change happening and/or when do we want to see results?

  ○ **Where** is it going to take place?

  ○ **HoW** are we going to make this happen?

  ○ **Why** — I save this one for last. It's an important part of change, however, it often gets left out or left behind. "Why?" Why are we doing this? While I don't have hard data, based on my experience, people forget to share the "why" because they know why. They just forget that the people with whom they are sharing the change don't know the why. They haven't been privy to conversations leading up to the decision to make the change. I've also discovered that even if people don't agree with the change, if they understand the reasoning behind it, they are more likely to support it. This question also helps us reflect on why we are doing something. I ask myself this often. Why am I really doing...?

- Ask for help.

- Give yourself and others time to adjust to the change, if possible.

- Keep the end goal in sight.

- Make a plan and work your plan.

- Look at what happened and why it happened. Consider all the consequences. Consider all the possibilities and alternatives. Don't get hung up on the obstacles. They can make you stronger and are learning opportunities.

- Talk through the changes with trusted peers and/or friends.

Remember: You don't have to be great to start, but you have to start to be great.

Your Reflection

Reflection Questions: Answer here or in a separate journal.

1. What change(s) am I facing now?

2. What changes do I control, and which ones do others control?

3. What is my biggest challenge with change?

4. What strategies do I use when dealing with change and what is one strategy I may want to use in the future when dealing with change?

Your Action Plan

Here is an example of what your action plan may look like. Remember it's your plan not mine, this is only an example to support you in getting started. Choose the action which will support you in moving forward. There is space for you to write your personal plan of action at the end of the example.

1. *Goal: To become more comfortable with change in general and specifically with a change in how we assess student learning in a capstone class.*

2. *Action: Take time to ask questions about the reason the change is happening. Consider the benefits in the long run to everyone involved. Keep a positive attitude. Figure out how I can be part of the change and make suggestions on how to implement the change if possible.*

3. *Who will support me? My peers*

4. *Date: December 2023*

5. *How will I know I'm making progress? I won't feel as anxious about change and will have answers to my questions. I will offer to be part of the solution when making the change and make suggestions on how to assess student learning.*

Your Turn: Answer here or in a separate journal.

1. Goal:

2. Action:

3. Who can support you?

4. Date to begin:

5. How will you know you made progress?

Your Biggest Take-away(s) Regarding Change

Caterpillars transform into beautiful butterflies in a season. Your transformation will be revealed in its own time. It may be a day, a week, a month, a season, or over years. Enjoy the journey. You will encounter many opportunities to change in life, some by choice, others created by those around us. Embrace change. Be as much a part of it as you are able. Have a vision and, like the caterpillar, keep growing because, "if you're not growing, you're dying." In order to support us with change, my friend the cat can share how staying curious, being patient, and taking care of yourself will help you in leading your team within.

Additional Resources

- Drew Dudley's TEDx—Lollipop Moments — I've heard of stories and movies that talk about the butterfly effect. You know how one change, an incident, or person affects another person's life or sets a chain of events in motion. Sometimes we know how we affect another person and many times, more often than not, we may never know the effect we have had on others. Yet, it's important to know you do influence others. Drew Dudley talks about lollipop moments in his TEDx. He talks about how one seemingly insignificant gesture changed a person's decision and possibly the course taken in life.

- *Start with Why* and *Find Your Why* by Simon Sinek.

- YouTube video https://www.youtube.com/watch?v=urntcMUJR9M (5 ways to lead in an era of constant change | Jim Hemerling (13 min)). He shares that when leading people through change it's important to put people first and focus on five ways to lead through change: 1) inspire through purpose, 2) go all in with initiatives 3) enable people with the capabilities they need to succeed in the transformation 4) instill a culture of continuous learning 5) have a vision with a clear roadmap and hold people accountable for results.

Change is hard. Change takes work. Change is inevitable.
Change—it's worth it!
"You can't change what you don't acknowledge."

Dr. Phil

The Cat

Curiosity, Patience, and Self-Care

"Why is patience so important? Because it makes us pay attention."

Paulo Coelho

𝓘t is said that "curiosity killed the cat"—but did it? I sure hope not, or my nine lives would be gone in a heartbeat.

I tend to drive people nuts with all of my questions, so I was surprised when the geese asked me to join the team. My friends and I work well together when it comes to decisions. They give you choices and I ask the questions to gather information to help you decide on which choice to focus. I'm also pretty good at encouraging you to remember things will work out; sometimes they just take time. I also want you to take care of yourself, which sounds like a simple task. For many, it's not.

Curiosity

Curiosity is one of my biggest strengths. I ask a lot of questions. In fact, *why* is one of my favorite words. Though it can drive people crazy. Do you know people who ask a lot of questions? Maybe you're the one who asks the questions. If you are—good for you!

So, what happens to us as adults when we hear a question beginning with the word "why?" Does it put you on the defensive? Based on Ann's experience, she believes it's because people think their thoughts, ability, answers, or decisions are being "questioned." In reality, she and I think people, most of the time, just want more information and a deeper, more in-depth understanding of the thinking behind a decision or opinion with whatever's going on, whether it's new policy or project, new store layout, or any type of change on which my friend the butterfly is an expert.

I've found sometimes people ask too many questions and other times they don't ask enough. Me, I'm super-curious about everything. Your behavior style—that is, whether you're driven, results oriented, direct, and fact oriented, or more social, people oriented, and laid back—can affect how you approach questions and how people perceive you when you ask them. I've heard Ann say several times that while she may still not agree with a change or policy, if she has a better understanding of it, it's easier to share with others and support it, as long as it's legal, ethical, and doesn't go against her core values.

Do you remember, or maybe your parents told you, when you were little, you were full of questions and nearly every sentence started with the word "why?" You asked questions because you were naturally curious and wanted to learn as much as you could about the world around you. If you have kids, nieces, nephews, grandkids, and so on, you're probably more than familiar with the "why" questions. Ever keep track of how many "why" questions they ask in a day? It's a lot. It's too bad so many get irritated with kiddos asking why. That's strange, because by asking questions, you can learn and grow.

Ann's son, Noah, constantly asked "why" and she loved it. How amazing it would be if people embraced the curiosity of a child instead of squelching it. It's an opportunity to support them in developing the ability to think and wonder, a quality I value and yet, how many times do you work to develop it in your own mind and in the minds of others?

As an adult, you might feel as if asking questions could be perceived as a weakness. I don't think it is. It's one of my superpowers. Ann likes to ask questions and as a Leadership and Team Coach, that's an excellent skill to have. She loves asking those tough questions with kindness and compassion. As an adult sometimes, depending on whom you're asking, how you're asking, and when you're asking the questions, you may be met with a variety of responses.

Sometimes it's a matter of reframing the question. I like all the "W" questions and work really hard to ask questions beginning with the other "Ws." I like the Who, What, When, Where, and hoW.

Sometimes it is a good idea to slow down and think things through. Slowing down doesn't mean a lack of progress or laziness, it just means you're taking time to rethink things or ask yourself or your peers those tough questions. "Am I or are we doing the right thing? Are you forging ahead before doing your due diligence in researching your product?"

It's important to ask others questions, too. Do you like to be told what to do? Most people don't. Ask questions and let the other person ask questions and work to figure out his or her own answer or way forward so they can come up with their own solution and buy into it. You also have the opportunity to say yes or no to the solutions discussed. Give others the same opportunity. It doesn't mean it's like this all the time, but we can at least ask questions and listen.

Asking questions helps you expand your thinking and gain the knowledge needed before you begin any type of project. There are some behavioral styles that ask more questions than others. I say let's embrace and encourage the questions.

Stay curious. The more questions you ask, the more you learn.

"If you can let go of passion and follow your curiosity, your curiosity just might lead you to your passion."

Elizabeth Gilbert

Patience

Ann prays for patience, and she'd like it right now. Can you relate? Do you want things to happen sooner rather than later? I get it, however when Ann takes time to think things through, ask questions, and consider all possibilities, she finds the result usually ends up better than if she would have just raced to the end.

Ann's cats (the real ones) are very patient like me, but that doesn't mean they aren't rowdy. They pounce on each other, their toys, and whatever else looks like fun to play with. How many times do you "pounce" on things or go after an idea before thinking things through? Ever spend money on a whim and ask yourself, "What was I thinking?" When if you'd taken time to ask a few more questions, you would have felt better about your decision? Even if it was the same decision. Have you ever hurriedly started a project without carefully looking at all the possibilities? Or at least listened to the team member(s) who asked more questions or had extra knowledge about the project?

Patience is tough to practice in a world with so much technology and social media. Instant gratification doesn't mean instant success. Overnight success usually takes 10–15 years. Ann's actual cats exhibit a great deal of patience like me. They will sit and watch for hours at a time, the leaves swirling around in a little whirlwind tornado like funnel on the patio, squirrels jumping from branch to branch chasing each other and chattering in a language only they understand, birds flitting from one tree to the next or making a nest in the wreath outside of the door, other cats freely roaming the neighborhood, and of course their little chipmunk friends who look at them through the sliding-glass door and laugh because they are outside and the cats are not.

Like Ann's cats I like to take my time to think things through and encourage you to do the same. It's important to take your time to get things right. It's also a good idea to give people the time they need, within reason, to think about an idea, make a decision, or work on a project.

"Patience is power. Patience is not an absence of action; rather, it is 'timing.' It waits on the right time to act, for the right principles and in the right way."

Fulton J. Sheen

Self-care

Leaders understand that taking care of themselves is important, yet many neglect it. I eat when I'm hungry, sleep when I'm tired, and have a keen eye to see things others don't. My team members wish I didn't take so many naps, and yet they know I encourage them to relax when they need it. How often do you take the time to relax? It's important to take a minute or two every once in a while, to take a deep breath, stretch, and clear your head so you can return to the project feeling refreshed with a new perspective. Ann doesn't really like to slow down, especially when she feels like she has a million things to do. Do you ever feel you're going 100 miles an hour and know you need to take a break yet don't because you don't have time or think you don't have time? Truth is, sometimes you don't have time not to.

Some team members may seem as if they are more interested in taking frequent breaks. They tend to be viewed as not being as "productive" as others are or as much as they could be. Yet when you're rested or in a place of calm, you may appreciate the beauty of your surroundings, ideas, and progress more than if you were overworked. It's not always about doing, but also being.

I like to relax by taking a nap, sometimes several during the day. Don't worry, I'm not suggesting you take a daily nap or two, especially while you're at work. I remind, and sometimes nag, you about taking care of yourself and the reason it's important. When you're tired, maybe it's your body's way of saying, slow down. Cause let's face it if you don't take care of yourself, you won't be around to take care of all the people and "things" you say are important to you. Some adults have a hard time relaxing, and others may relax a little too much. It's painful trying to hit that happy medium.

Our kids take naps to re-energize, even though they resist lying down to rest. Most adults do a great job of taking care of their kiddos and yet don't take enough time to take care of themselves.

Are you thinking that you want and need to take better care of yourself? Whether it's eating healthier, being more active (I say that because Ann doesn't like to exercise), doing more things you enjoy (maybe volunteering, reading, biking, etc.) or spending more time with family and friends. It's important to carve out free time, even when it's tough.

Keeping an appointment with yourself to exercise, taking a mental-health break, spending time with your family, friends, or yourself is critical. If you take care of yourself, you will be in a healthy state to take care of the people and things that are important to you. Self-care isn't selfish. It's selfless. If you make a conscious decision to do it, you can do it. It's important. It's necessary.

I bet you can see the reason the geese invited me to the team.

"If you take care of yourself, you'll be around to take care of others. If you don't. You won't"

Unknown

The Bus. The Breakdown. The Questions.

Ann is no stranger to questions. Little did Ann know when she began asking questions at a young age, it was just the beginning of a lifetime asking questions and a curious mindset. When she was around 12, her family went to Walt Disney World. Sunday, they boarded an old double-decker bus that would take them to a church in Kissimmee, 30 miles away from Disney World. She and her sisters wanted to go straight to Disney World. However, her parents worked hard to instill the importance of attending church each Sunday—a habit she would lose in her twenties, only to return to in her thirties. Now, instead of "having" to go, she "gets" to go to church, but that's a story for another book.

I'm sure you're wondering, what does this have to do with curiosity? Well, after church, on an extremely hot and humid Sunday in July, the bus broke down on the way back to Disney World, much to the dismay of the 60-plus people on the bus. While they all waited impatiently for taxis to come pick them up and return them to Disney, most of the passengers sat in their seats, working to figure out how to pass the time. I'd like to note this was way before cell phones so no games, no texts, no internet to search for random topics. They had to figure out how to pass the time the old-fashioned way—using their imaginations.

Much to her mom's chagrin, Ann decided she would get to know the other people on the bus. And she meant all the people on the bus, one family, one person, one conversation at a time. She visited several people and would then return to her family and "report" what she learned about the people with whom she had a conversation. She shared where they were from, if they had pets, what they did for a living. You get the picture. You name it and she asked it. Her Mom said no one really wanted to talk to her and answer all her questions because they were hot and just wanted to get back to Disney World. Ann confidently shared with her mom, "Of course they want to talk to me; they're answering all my questions." Hence, I supported her in learning to ask questions and develop her sense of curiosity. Little did she know then that would support her goal of talking with people in the Jaycees, as a coach, a friend, and working on her own podcast where she will ask powerful questions to guests and listeners and together, they will discover practical solutions.

Joe is Funny and Curious

Ann met Joe through ICF Iowa. Their relationship grew when they each found themselves in Mitch Matthews' Acceleration Mastermind, as well as the Perceptions workshop hosted by Mitch and Travis. Joe's superpower is his ability to think quickly on his feet. If you want someone for improv, Joe is your person!

Joe's biggest struggle is his curiosity, which came as a surprise to her. Perhaps many struggle with it. Joe used to be a project manager. Sometimes when working on a project with his team, the end goal either changed or some team members didn't know the end goal. Joe worked to encourage his team to dig deep and ask the hard questions that fostered engagement and created trust among team members. He discovered that even though it may be uncomfortable and challenging to ask tough questions, not asking was doing a disservice to not only himself but also his team. You may not know all the answers yet, but by asking questions and being curious, you give yourself the opportunity to discover answers. You might not find all the answers, but by not asking the questions, it's a given you won't get the information for which you are searching.

Be curious and have deep conversations. It builds trust and understanding among friends and team members.

New Jaycee Chapters

Ann and her peers helped many people in a variety of Iowa towns begin Jaycee chapters that would host projects to serve their communities. Jeff, one of Ann's mentors and good friends, asked her how she remembered so many details of the people to whom they talked, since it usually took two to three times talking with them over several days or weeks, before they joined the new chapter. She shared with him she took notes on little index cards (remember, no fancy cell phones to record notes). People want to know you care about them as people and not just as a number or check. Similar to when Mark at Holmes Oldsmobile, where Ann bought her car, kept notes about their conversations. No, not creepy notes, but notes about where she worked and so on. I'm sure he looked at them prior to when they met about her buying a car, which was every five or six years. The point of this is, he was curious from a customer-service standpoint, kept notes, and let her know her business was important to him, and she wasn't just a transaction. We could use a little more curiosity and interest in our customers today.

Mrs. Warner and the Second Grade

Ann loved Mrs. Warner, her second-grade teacher. She instilled a love of books and reading in Ann. She also most likely played a major role in Ann's need to feel productive every second of every minute of every day.

Mrs. Warner had her students doing something every second, of every minute, of every day. Granted, when you have a room full of second-graders, it's probably a good idea to keep them occupied. When they were finished with an assignment, project, or book, they could not just sit there for a couple minutes. They were expected to get another book and keep busy. They kept reading records that tracked how many books they read, which probably contributed to Ann having more books than she will ever be able to read.

To this day, Ann has a hard time doing nothing or doing things that "seem" unproductive. Though what may seem "unproductive" is actually very important and crucial in being productive in life.

It's important and okay to take a break and relax. By taking a break, she realized she is actually more productive when she gets enough sleep, does Wordle, takes time to work on a jigsaw puzzle, or sits outside on the patio having a glass of wine, enjoying the outdoors, and a conversation with her husband or friends.

Relationships and self-care are critical to maintaining your mental health. Ann has a plaque with a saying on it, "Enjoy the little things in life for someday you'll look back and realize they were the big things." This already rings true.

You may laugh, but Ann's family took Mrs. Warner and Mrs. Barnes, Ann's first-grade teacher, homemade Christmas cookies every year until she was a senior in high school. I know she wished they were both alive so she could tell them what a positive impact they made in her life.

Bed Rest and Preterm Labor: Self-Care and Patience

When Ann was pregnant, taking care of herself was a top priority for her. Little did she know that would serve well when she went into preterm labor at 29 weeks. For someone who didn't sleep eight hours a night and was constantly on the go, how would she ever have the patience to be on bed rest for the remainder of her pregnancy? That thought concerned Doug, too, because he knew Ann was a workaholic like her dad. Truth be told, she still is, but not to the same extent as she used to be. He was curious about the hospital stay and asked whether she would be in the hospital for the remaining 10ish weeks. The doctor's answer, "Our goal is to get her to 32 weeks." While it was only seven short days until Noah arrived, the patience it took to be on bed rest didn't compare to the patience it took during the 52 days he hung out in the NICU (Neonatal Intensive Care Unit) until he went home. Patience is easier to find when you focus on the end goal. Here, taking a healthy baby home took priority over everything. In the workplace, it might be finding the information needed to complete a project.

Lessons Learned

- It's okay to be curious. Questions come in all shapes and sizes. It's not always easy to be curious, patient, and practice self-care, and yet it is important and doable if you make a conscious choice to do it.

- Keep your sense of wonder.

- The questions you ask yourself need to be important and relevant to your own unique situation.

- If you need a break, take one—whether it's a physical one or a mental one. Take a catnap now and then. It's not selfish to take care of yourself and encourage others to take care of themselves. Many people work long days. Sometimes it's not the hours but the work itself. Eight, 10, 12-hour days. That may work for a few days, but there comes a time where your productivity isn't there.
- Life gets busy. Listen to your body and your sixth sense, the little voice inside of you. Stop, relax, and enjoy life.
- Take care of yourself so you can take care of others. If you don't take care of yourself—who will? Remember to stop and smell the roses.

My Strengths

- Staying curious and asking questions.
- Patience.
- Self-care.

Your Strengths (List the strengths you see in yourself when it comes to curiosity, patience, and self-care.)

Strategies: Choose the one(s) which will best serve you.

- Breathe.
- Journal — If you think it, ink it. Putting it in writing can support you in sorting out your thoughts and feelings. Self-reflection can help clarify what's going on.
- Take time for yourself and do something which brings you joy. Read a book. Have lunch with a friend. Do a puzzle.
- Stay active. Take a walk.

- Pray.

- Ask powerful questions for a deeper understanding and to help others work to figure out the solutions that are best for them. Use as many "W" questions *(Who, What, When, Where, and hoW.)* as you can without using the word "Why"—it puts people on the defensive.

  ○ For example, instead of asking, "Why did you use this strategy?" Consider saying something like, "What were some of the reasons that inspired you to choose this strategy?" Or "Would you share more about the strategies so I have a better understanding of them or so I can help others in better understanding?" The "W" questions like, Who, What, When, Where, and How work well. Sometimes, "Why" is hard to avoid, and yet you can ask almost any question starting with something other than the word "Why." Work to change the "why" to a "what" question.

  ○ Learn what you are thinking as well as what others are thinking. This is important with kids, too. As a parent, grandparent, aunt, uncle, guardian or trusted adult, one of the most important things you can do, and one of the hardest, is to listen— really listen to what your kiddos are saying. By the way, depending on the age, let them talk through solutions. If they buy into the solutions, they are more likely to follow through. Besides, do you like to be told what to do? Me neither. Most would rather be part of the decision and change than let it happen to them. With boys growing up, talk in the car—it's easier to talk if you don't have to look at the person all the time. Eye contact is important and so is side-by-side when you're connecting with your son(s).

- Think before moving forward.
- Make and take time to rest, even if it's a brief break, whether it is mental or physical.
- Eat well—eat a healthy snack. Ann includes a piece of dark chocolate once in a while.
- Drink lots of water.
- Take a catnap.
- Learn something new. Take a class.
- Spend time with yourself—ask yourself the hard questions whether they be for your personal or professional life.
  - What do I want to pursue?
  - What is important to me?
  - Does what I'm doing match my values?
- Get out of your house and out of your own head. Do you need a change of venue? With so many people working at home, sometimes the lines between your personal and professional lives are blurred. Go to the library or a coffee shop to work—you're away from your normal environment and some of the distractions at home or the office.
- Change how you do things. Use a mind-map for outlining projects, a book, or ideas. It can be useful for many things when you feel stuck. It may help you get "unstuck."

Your Reflection

Reflection Questions: Answer here or in a separate journal.

1. How comfortable am I asking questions?

2. How can I take better care of myself?

3. How patient of a person am I and what pushes my buttons and causes me to be impatient?

4. What gives me cause to pause and observe what's happening around me?

Your Biggest Take-away(s) Regarding Curiosity, Patience, and Self-Care

Your Action Plan

Here is an example of what your action plan may look like. Remember it's your plan not mine, this is only an example to support you in getting started. Choose the action which will support you in moving forward. There is space for you to write your personal plan of action at the end of the example.

1. *Goal: To become more active and take better care of myself*

2. *Who will support me? My husband and Marci*

3. *Action: Walk for 20 minutes a day at least four times/ week (Target days — Monday, Wednesday, Friday, and one weekend day)*

4. *Date: Begin June 1, 2023*

5. *How will I know I'm making progress? I will track my progress in my calendar.*

Your Turn: Answer here or in a separate journal.

1. Goal:

2. Action:

3. Who can support you?

4. Date to begin:

5. How will you know you made progress?

Curiosity didn't kill the cat. Ignoring one's questions and one's self can kill an idea or a spirit. Stay curious, be patient and take care of yourself. Stop and smell the roses. The dove, who you'll meet next, is a master of taking time to not only smell the roses, but to help all of us find inner peace and contentment.

Additional Resources

- *The Advice Trap* by Michael Bungay Stanier.
- "The Advice Monster" TED Talk by Michael Bungay Stanier.
- *Mindset* by Carol Dwyer.
- *Play Your Bigger Game* by Rick Tamlyn.

The Dove

Peace

"God, grant me the serenity to accept the things I cannot change, the courage to change the things I can, and the wisdom to know the difference."

Attributed to Reinhold Niebuhr

*I*s finding and feeling a sense of peace important to you? Does peace elude you? Overall, in life, I have found people want a certain element of peace and contentment in their lives. I think people want that in a career too. I know there's always going to be a certain level of stress and angst; however, my role is to bring as much peace and harmony to you and your team as possible. I'm your dove and the voice on the team that assures everyone that no matter what happens, things will eventually work out.

Even when things don't work out the way you want or think they "should," I do my best to be the voice that shares the sense you did the best you could. It's time to accept what is and move on with a sense of peace. Some think I may keep peace at all costs. I don't mind conflict, yet when people hear that word, they usually cringe. I handle conflict in the right manner to make it productive. Since many team members have different ideas and differences of opinions, there is a good chance we will reach the best solution possible and eventually find peace in the decision and within ourselves.

My job is to support you and bring a calm confidence to you and the team. I work tirelessly to remind you to quiet yourself not only on the outside but on the inside, too. I am soft-spoken. Some say the one who speaks, or whispers softly, is most often the one to whom people listen. Achieving peace within yourself can be like that: soft and silent, yet strong at the same time. Strength can come from handling situations with grace and accepting what is finally decided and moving on without holding a grudge.

It's important to keep all team members working together and to maintain peace and harmony on the inside and out. Heck, sometimes it's easier to keep peace on the outside than within yourself. I'm also the part of your team who helps each person to have a voice.

When Ann facilitates workshops, she talks about the team member who brings patience and a sense of calmness to the team. You know, the one that can take a deep breath and assure everyone that everything will work out if everyone listens to each other and works together. I can instill a quiet peace and calmness in an otherwise chaotic environment. Calm and being relaxed are not feelings which come easy for Ann. Anybody have a lot of nervous energy or know anyone who does? You may benefit from a lot of energy in many areas, but not when trying to relax or if a calm approach is necessary. The good news? There is a dove waiting to be unleashed in all of you. You just may need to give me space and work on consciously being calm.

Peace means different things to different people. It comes in various forms throughout the seasons of life. In the early stages of Ann's career, peace came from knowing she was moving toward a leadership position in the organization for which she worked. In her thirties, it was finding love and enjoying a relationship with the possibility of having a family. When her first marriage ended in divorce, she thought I left her and went on a vacation. In reality, she sent me on a vacation. I was always there. She just didn't listen to me.

I returned when Ann had had enough of the chaos and returned to church.

Upon returning to church (though you have to decide where peace lives in you) she began to regain her peace of mind and heart, and I resurfaced. Getting married again and having a family, peace came in, making them a priority over work. Now, Ann finds peace in remembering and acting on what is truly important to her. It's not something given, it's something you create within yourself. It's a feeling of contentment. It's having all of the "team" working in sync and appreciating what they bring to the table.

You gain peace by enjoying what you have, not worrying about what you don't have or what you think you want. This new mindset brings her a new sense of freedom and inner contentment. Don't worry, I know it's not as easy as I'm making it sound, especially with all the things pulling at you personally and professionally as well as all the messages about what success looks like, sent to you daily, compliments of society and social media.

Peace today might look different than it did yesterday, last week, last year, or a decade ago. It can change with the different seasons life holds. When you're young, peace might be going out on Friday or Saturday night. As you get older, it might be a quiet night hanging out with friends at someone's house or even time spent with yourself, reading a book, enjoying a hobby, or working on a jigsaw puzzle. Is it challenging for you to feel and find peace and contentment in life? What about at work?

What are some ways that people are challenged in finding peace?

- Letting others define what success is for them.
- Comparing yourself to others.
- Too much social media.

It's important to remember it's not about what peace means to others; it's about what peace means to you. I'm not by any means saying to ignore what others need, that's not it at all. What I mean is, besides taking care of others, it's important to find peace and contentment within yourself. It may be knowing you're doing the best you can at any given moment in time.

> *"The grass isn't greener on the other side. It is just a different color green."*
>
> *Ann Wright*

Ann's Continued Search for Inner Peace

Inner peace does not come easy for Ann. Her ambition played tricks on her. Allowing society to define success hindered her in the past. She finally realized she needed to figure out what was important to her and how she defined success. She then began working toward achieving it. Ann thought I would be easy to write about, but as it turns out, for her I am perhaps the hardest one to talk about because I am the one she struggles with the most—finding peace on the inside. Ann knows I am one team member who works overtime for her. She is not a calm person by nature. She has a lot of energy and enthusiasm, which is a blessing and a curse. It's a blessing because she can accomplish a great deal. It can be a curse because too much energy sometimes annoys people or makes them nervous.

Real peace for Ann is knowing and remembering that she is enough. I am the reflection of her innermost thoughts, the lens into her soul, and who she wants to see looking back at her in the mirror. She doesn't have to be *the best*. She just needs to be *her* best—the best version of herself that she can be on any given day. That's really all any of us can be.

Her son asked recently, "How do you know what's good enough? Can't I always do better?"

That is a tough question. Ann grew up hearing, "do your best," and worked to instill that sentiment in Noah and to strive for a sense of pride or desire to be proud of the person you are and your accomplishments. When is it good enough? Not only does Ann wish she had the answer to this question, but so do I as your team member who brings you peace. Ann thinks it's when you know in your heart you have done the best you can do with the knowledge and skills you have. It's like this book. There is a sense of peace knowing she finally wrote and published it. She did the best she could at a certain point in time. She is looking forward to writing the next one and putting to use all the things she's learned along the way in writing this one.

Ann has many interests and loves to be involved in things. Because she likes to be involved, she says, "yes," to too many things or activities. While it seems like a wonderful decision, she often ends up overcommitting and is, at times, stressed with being too busy and not taking enough time for her faith, family, friends, and self. Ever enjoy all the things you are doing, but then find you don't have time to just relax? That's exactly the feeling this lesson refers to.

After her son graduated from high school, she toyed with the idea of not taking on any additional responsibilities for a full year. Sometimes she wishes she had stuck to this, and other times she is glad she didn't. With the desire to expand her coaching and training practice, she knew it would be important to be involved with a variety of activities.

She loved serving on the ICF Iowa Board of Directors. By being on the Board, she had the opportunity to serve the chapter and stay focused on coaching. The experience has given her the chance to meet coaches from around the world and stay up to date on some of the latest trends in the coaching industry. At work, this brings her peace. Ann is happier, more productive, kinder, and more patient when she feels peace and when the team is in sync with each other.

Ann has two mourning doves who live in her backyard in spring and summer. They take off in the winter because let's face it—Iowa winters are harsh. There are winters she wishes she could leave for about three months, traveling south just like the birds do. In the quiet of the early morning, just seeing them and if the windows are open hearing them, can bring a sense of peacefulness, if only for a moment.

Julie and Her Peace Practices

Julie and Ann met at a weekend workshop. Immediately drawn to her peaceful aura, Ann knew they would stay connected no matter the miles between them. Julie works for the organization known as *Memos from the Head Office*. She is intuitive, displays empathy to all, feels deeply, and loves unconditionally. Julie is one of the calmest and most peaceful people Ann knows. Bringing a sense of peace to every person and situation she encounters; she also possesses the unique gift of being able to receive them. She sees them the way they were created. When sharing insights with someone, it's almost like a chiropractic adjustment, realigning and shifting things into their divine intent. Julie senses where they are and on what they can focus to accomplish their goals. For Ann, she brings calm to the chaos, which helps her remember to take a breath, refocus, and take actions that will move her closer to achieving her goals.

Ann recently asked her what she did to achieve and maintain peace among the craziness in the world, especially when life throws you a curveball. For example, Julie and her husband have traveled the United States in a motorhome, working to determine where they wanted to put down their roots. California is where they settled. Faith in God and his plan guides Julie in her decisions. They moved into a home and transformed their motor home into an Airbnb on ten acres of land in wine country in Southern California.

Things looked as if they were finally falling into place. They were then informed they would have to move as the owners of the home in which they were staying were moving back home and into their house. With approximately one month to find a new place, it would have been so easy to feel anger and frustration. Like Julie shared, there's a lot of anger out there. However, it's up to us to create the peace we want and deserve.

Julie is a "Peace Releaser." To calm the chaos, and feel the presence of God's loving hand, she works to remember the following scripture, "Greater is he who is in you than he who is in the world" (1 John 4:4 NASB).

Her mantra? Figure out what you can and need to do to influence a shift in the environment in the room in which you enter. Your words and actions can make a difference.

As Julie practices what she preaches and releases, she continues to have faith and does not allow the uncertainty of life to be a burden. Julie works to shed light on things! She knows it sounds a bit mysterious, but everything she does is done in love! She uses her *Peace Practices,* which are listed below.

1. Take deep breaths.
2. Listen to your internal dialogue—shift it; change it; be aware of your self-talk. (Check out the Parrot chapter if you haven't already.)

3. Connect with nature—take a walk, sit on the deck or patio, get some fresh air.

4. Figure out what works for you. Embrace it. Impart it on others as appropriate.

5. Take charge of yourself.

6. Acknowledge how you feel. Determine how you want to feel. Decide the strategies you will use. Take action. Keep working until you achieve the peace you want and deserve.

Julie and Ann have similar outlooks on life. Both hope you find peace in your day and calm in any storm. Julie was quick to share that it's important for everyone to find and define their own "peace practices." Ann and I totally agree. While this book provides ideas and strategies, it's not all-inclusive. Find what works for you and do it. If at any time it's not working, re-evaluate and find something that does. After each storm, there is a rainbow. For Ann, this is God's way of saying life goes on. The pot of gold at the end of the rainbow is different for everyone—figure out what's important to you and go for it. Find your personal pot of gold which may likely look much different than the next person's gold. It might include:

- Living the single life
- Traveling
- Friends
- Family
- Career
- Time to yourself

Below are a few suggestions from Julie on how to discover your own peace of mind and pot of gold, though are by no means the only ways to find it.

- Take time to think about and put on paper your personal values.

- Write out your goals and priorities.
- Determine what success looks and feels like to you. It's different for everyone.
- Journal about a time you felt peace within yourself.

Lessons Learned

- Be happy with who you are.
- You are enough.
- Find peace and freedom in knowing it's okay to say no to things, because when you say no to one thing, you're saying yes to something else.
- You can find harmony, peace, and contentment in different ways at different times in your life.
- Peace looks and feels different for different people. It's up to you to determine what peace and contentment mean to you. For many, it includes achieving balance and alignment between home and work life and making certain what you're doing aligns with your values. There are no right or wrong answers.
- Different things at different times in your life will bring you peace and contentment. Acknowledge what brings you peace and work toward it.
- Find peace in your day and calm among any storm. Remember, after the storm there is a rainbow, which for Ann is God's way of saying life goes on. The pot of gold at the end of the rainbow is different for everyone. Figure out what's important to you and what brings you peace and go for it.

My Strengths

- Calming the chaos
- Supporting you in finding peace of mind and peace within your heart.

Your Strengths (List the strengths you see in yourself when it comes to finding inner peace.)

Strategies: Choose the one(s) which will best serve you.

- Pray, if you choose. For Ann, she works to remember that God is in control. Her faith helps give her peace.

- Talk to trusted friends.

- Surround yourself with positive people.

- Keep a journal. Write about what's going well and what you want to do more or less of that will bring you peace and contentment in your life.

- Define your own success and what inner peace means to you.

- Limit time on social media—very little of what you see on social media is as it appears.

- Take time for yourself—self-care matters.

- Phone a friend.

- Text a friend—let them know you are thinking of them. Sometimes focusing on others helps you.

- Listen to your internal dialogue—shift it; change it; be aware of your self-talk. (Check out the Parrot chapter if you haven't already.)

- Figure out what inner peace looks and feels like for you. Embrace it. Impart it on others as appropriate.

- Take charge of yourself.

- Acknowledge how you feel. Determine how you want to feel. Decide the strategies you will use. Take action. Keep working until you achieve the peace you want and deserve.

- Connect with nature—take a walk, sit on the deck or patio, get some fresh air (Julie).

Your Reflection

Reflection Questions: Answer here or in a separate journal.

1. What brings me peace? (At home? At work?)
2. When do I feel most at peace and how does it feel?

Your Biggest Take-Away(s) Regarding Finding Peace

Your Action Plan

Here is an example of what your action plan may look like. Remember it's your plan not mine, this is only an example to support you in getting started. Choose the action which will support you in moving forward. There is space for you to write your personal plan of action at the end of the example.

1. *Goal: To feel more content in life*
2. *Action: Say a quick prayer in the morning. It will include three things. 1. Thank God for something or the people in my life. 2. Ask for help with something. 3. Pray for someone.*
3. *Who will support me? Patty. I will also wear my cross necklace as a reminder to do this daily.*
4. *Date: September 3*
5. *How will I know I'm making progress? I will feel more at peace with myself. It won't mean that circumstances have changed on the outside, but I will feel more content on the inside.*

Your Turn: Answer here or in a separate journal.

1. Goal:

2. Action:

3. Who can support you?

4. Date to begin:

5. How will you know you made progress?

It takes confidence to look at the other side and realize it is or isn't what we really want. In order to help with confidence my friend the eagle, who soars to great heights, is going to share a little about how to find and continue developing your confidence in the next chapter.

Additional Resources

- *The Pray Powered Entrepreneur* by Kim Avery.
- *Finding Joy* by Carrie Copley.

The Eagle
Confidence

*"The race is not always to the swift... but to those
who keep on running."*

*D*o you ever have days when you are confident and feel as if you can conquer the world and whatever life throws at you? Are there other days or times you're like, good grief, I don't know if I can do this or not, and you feel defeated before you even get started? Do you ever feel your confidence is (or is going to end up) on the endangered-species list? I know how that feels. I was on that list, too.

I, the bald eagle, have been the national bird of the United States since 1782. And I was *still* on the endangered species list. The United States finally removed me from that list in August 2007. However, I am still protected under the Migratory Bird Treaty Act and the Bald and Golden Eagle Protection Act.

That means I'm the team member who will support and protect you when your confidence is rattled and gets put on your own endangered species list.

Confidence can be tricky to find and understand. Sometimes you feel confident that you know what you're doing and have what you need to accomplish your goal. You feel good about yourself. It doesn't mean you know it all. Because let's face it. Nobody knows everything about anything. However, it's about knowing that with the right resources, knowledge, skills, other team members, and processes, you and your team can accomplish the goals you set out to achieve.

How does your confidence make it onto the endangered species list?

Your confidence can waver during moments when you aren't sure you have the knowledge or skills needed for the job or whatever it is you're doing. Other times it's because someone has said something to or about you, which causes you to doubt yourself.

What can you do to develop more self-confidence?

If you need increased knowledge or skills for a job, research where you can acquire what you need and enroll in classes to learn and develop those skills.

Some people find and develop self-confidence through the support of family and friends, those who will be honest, kind, tell it like it is and will share what needs to be done in an encouraging and positive way. Others find it through their faith in God, knowing that he will provide what they need. Dig deep and you will discover the courage to ask questions and know that through a multitude of experiences and perseverance, you will develop confidence even when things don't always go your way. Continue learning and growing through reading books and experimenting with strategies. Knowing what doesn't work is sometimes as powerful as knowing what does.

I have also found that having the strength to ask yourself if what was said to or about you is true or is it just someone's perspective because you're different from them is key. Are they saying it to hurt you or to help you grow? If multiple people make the same comment, it's probably a good idea to examine what was said and determine if a change is needed. Change takes strength and confidence, so give yourself a pat on the back for having the confidence to ask yourself some hard questions and examine the answers.

Help others develop their confidence and in turn, you will be developing yours at the same time.

Through having interviewed for jobs, interviewing hundreds of people for *other* jobs, and having taught interviewing skills to members of her team, Ann knows that one of the most common interview questions asked is none other than, "What are your strengths?"

We know it's coming, but it's a tough question to answer because most people don't want to feel as if they are "bragging." It takes confidence and self-awareness to know what your strengths are and share your strengths as well as weaknesses during an interview.

Interviewers ask this question because they want to know— do you know what your strengths are and how are those strengths going to help them reach their goals? They also want to do the best they can in hiring the right person for the job. People are sometimes hesitant to share their strengths in an interview, as they don't want to appear cocky or arrogant. However, this is your time to shine. Be confident and comfortable sharing what knowledge and skills you bring to this potential employer and have to offer the team. Ann's friend, Mitch Matthews, shares that it's not bragging if it's true. Share your strengths with confidence.

By the way, if you don't get the job, it just means it wasn't the right fit. Don't let it cause you to question yourself or influence your self-confidence. There's nothing wrong with you. The right job will happen, you just have to keep trying and draw on your turtle team member who will help you with perseverance, the parrot for some positive self-talk, and your support system who will remind you of all the positives you offer.

Strength and sheer determination can help you to develop confidence or regain and build it when it waivers. The hardest limitations are the ones you place on yourself. Only you can set aside or eliminate them. Dig deep and find the strength and confidence to keep going. Work to squash the imposter syndrome, which shows up to rob you of your confidence.

I know this is a cliché, but it's true. "When the going gets tough, the tough get going." If this were easy, everyone would be doing it. It takes strength, internal fortitude, strength, and confidence to make the choice to forge ahead, sometimes into the unknown.

Let me, your eagle, fly and let your confidence soar.

Doug Moves and Begins a New Career in a New City

Moving from a small town of one thousand people to Des Moines, Iowa with more than 250,000 people can be daunting.

Doug, Ann's husband, did exactly that. He decided after dating her long distance for two years that if they were going to see if the relationship was going to work, he would need to move closer to her. He took a leap of faith and moved.

Where would the confidence come from to make this move?

While change can be challenging and confidence scarce, when facing the unknown, he had faced the unfamiliar before in much of his time with the Jaycees, an organization focused on leadership training through community service. Knowing that finding a place to live, starting a new career, and going back to school would be a major change in his life and take a tremendous amount of work, he relied on his leadership experience with the Jaycees to help him with the confidence to make all those changes. Relying on the support of friends, the desire to elevate his career and skills also provided him with the strength and determination to be successful in this next chapter of his life.

With a background in farming, he took a job as a crop insurance agent. After a short six months, he realized and found the courage and confidence to admit he didn't care for sales. Hence, the search for a different job began—again. Before looking for a new career, he made a list of his strengths and skills so he would be prepared and confident in the interviews. With his background in farming and insurance experience, he landed a position as a crop insurance underwriter. Confidence grew as his knowledge base and experience in the business grew. He earned his bachelor's degree, and he was promoted. He's enjoyed a career as a crop insurance underwriter ever since.

The Mammography Bill: Confidence and Determination

Working with Tom Miller, one of Iowa's most successful and longest-running Attorney Generals, part of Ann's job with the American Cancer Society was to lobby at the State Capitol. The mammography bill could not have come at a better or worse time for Ann. Shortly before the legislative session, which began in January, Ann's first husband announced that he didn't know if wanted to stay married.

The Sunday after Thanksgiving, he announced that he didn't know if he ever loved her. This shook her self-confidence to the core. They separated just after Christmas and "dated" for a few months. (He filed for a divorce in late spring and papers were served just before their third anniversary.) Navigating a divorce Ann didn't want took a great deal of work, self-examination, and determination.

Determination came in the form of not letting grief or disappointment define her or change the essence of who she was. She made the decision to allow the experience, no matter how painful and unwanted, to make her a better, more understanding, and empathetic person as opposed to becoming bitter. Through counseling, a lot of work on herself, and much support from family and close friends, she regained her self-confidence and worth and made it through the experience.

This experience would cause her to be there for friends who would endure their own painful divorces in the years to come. While it was a challenge to go through it, she got through it and so did her friends because of their own determination and strength! They are some of the most confident women she knows. All of them, Ann included, still experience a lack of confidence from time to time. They're human. However, because they rely on their inner strength, and each other, they are determined to meet any obstacle that gets in their way.

Back to the mammography bill.

This bill came at a tough time because Ann's self-confidence was at an all-time low. She questioned whether she had the strength, stamina, knowledge, and skills to convince legislators it was a good idea to have insurance cover mammograms. Prevention is by far less costly than treatment, however it's not a concept accepted by all. It's better today than it was, but we still have a long way to go.

The bill came at a good time because it gave her purpose—a purpose to pass a bill that would provide the means for women to have mammograms that could detect breast cancer in its early stages, hence saving lives. By focusing on others and the mammography bill, it gave her a break from being too self-absorbed in her own situation, at least throughout the day. It gave her a sense of being part of something bigger than herself and a larger purpose.

Noah and the Broken Leg

One of the hardest things a parent must do is to watch their child struggle.

Noah broke his leg from an accidental fall a couple of weeks after his third birthday. He fell less than six inches from a little shopping cart shaped like a truck. One spiral fracture later, he found himself in a full lower-body cast for five and a half weeks.

At three, he experienced the two- and three-year-old milestones for the second time after the cast was removed. He had to learn to crawl, stand, climb stairs, and walk all over again. It would have been extremely easy for Ann to carry him from room to room or up the stairs, especially when he asked her in his sweet little voice and looked up at her with his big green eyes. However, it would have taken him twice as long to learn everything again and build his confidence if Ann and her husband had done everything for him.

One of the hardest moments came in February when he struggled to climb the stairs from the basement playroom to the kitchen and asked to be carried. Ann simply said, "I know you can do this on your own. I'm right behind you."

His challenge and success brought tears to their eyes, first watching him struggle to make it up the stairs (she was, of course, right behind him) and second, when he made it up the stairs by himself. One of the most rewarding and proudest moments for Ann and Doug is when Noah turned and said, "I did it!"

Helping to instill a sense of independence, pride in what one accomplishes, and that "can do" attitude is important for children, so they take it with them into adulthood. It's much easier to learn and practice as a child rather than to have to learn it as an adult. To this day Noah has the confidence to try different things.

Lessons Learned

- When your confidence is strong and you feel good about yourself, it is so much easier to tackle the obstacles life puts in front of you, finish projects needing your attention, and work hard to accomplish your goals.

- When things are tough and your confidence wavers, it takes effort. Sometimes a little. Sometimes a lot.

- You have what it takes to succeed.

- Confidence. It's one key to success. It's about believing in yourself and having the strength to remain confident in your abilities to handle life as you know it.

- You have the strength to dig deep inside yourself and invest the time and hard work it takes to get where you want to be.

- It is through the most challenging of times that you can build, regain, or maintain your self- confidence.

- Hold on to what you want and what's important to you. Let me take you places you never thought possible but always dreamed of reaching. Every dream is possible. Stop comparing yourself to others. Dream your dreams, not someone else's. Believe in yourself—you got this. Now go soar higher than you thought that you could!

- Be yourself! Don't try to be anyone but yourself— everyone else is taken.

- Pause. Listen. Think. Determine which path to take.

- Confidence can be fueled with the knowledge and wisdom gained in life.

- Remember your why—this will help you when you need strength.

My Strengths

- Confidence
- Determination

Your Strengths (List the strengths you see in yourself when it comes to self-confidence.)

Strategies: Choose the one(s) which will best serve you.

How do you develop and keep your confidence and strength? What are strategies you can use and share with others to discover your strength and confidence?

- Reach out and ask (email or in-person) three to five trusted peers/friends if they will share five positive qualities/characteristics they see in you. Keep those in a place where you can see them or access them daily, especially when your confidence is wavering.

- Write about a time you felt confident about something. Include how you felt and why you felt confident. Look at it from time to time, especially in the tough times.

- Call someone who will have a positive and honest conversation with you—not tell you what you want to hear or what to do, but talk it through with you and support you in drawing your own conclusions.

- Think about a couple of people who you believe have self-confidence. How do they act? What words do they use? What tone of voice do they use?

- What traits do you want to emulate from others while still being true to yourself?

- Write down your dreams, goals, and strengths.

- Continue gaining different experiences.

- Practice that in which you want to excel.

- Continue learning.

- Keep up that positive self-talk.

- Get an accountability buddy.

- Surround yourself with positive people.

- Work with a coach.

Your Reflection

Reflection Questions: Answer here or in a separate journal.

1. When do I feel the most/least confident?

2. What could I do to increase my self-confidence?

3. What am I doing to protect my self-confidence?

Your Biggest Takeaway(s) Regarding Self-Confidence

Your Action Plan

Here is an example of what your action plan may look like. Remember it's your plan not mine, this is only an example to support you in getting started. Choose the action which will support you in moving forward. There is space for you to write your personal plan of action at the end of the example.

1. *Goal: To be more confident*

2. *Action: Ask three to five trusted people what they see as my strengths as well as make a list of what I see as my strengths. I will also keep a list of my strengths where I can easily refer to it when my confidence waivers. I am also going to write about a time when I felt confident and the reasons for my confidence. This will help me remember I have knowledge and skills that are valuable. I am also going to keep learning about writing and publishing books by continuing to work with my book coach and Self-Publishing.com where there is a wealth of information and training about the self-publishing industry.*

3. *Who will support me? My three to five trusted friends, the self-publishing organization, and my coach.*

4. *Date: August 1*

5. *How will I know I'm making progress? I will have the list from my trusted friends and put it in a place where I can easily refer to it. I will feel more confident on the inside when I make a decision or comment and remember that all opinions have value, even if people don't agree with me or value mine. I will publish books two and three.*

Your Turn: Answer here or in a separate journal.

1. Goal:

2. Action:

3. Who can support you?

4. Date to begin:

5. How will you know you made progress?

The 'C' words just keep poppin up and play a huge role in the area of confidence. In this case communication, conflict, and conversations are the ones that come to mind. My good friend the elephant, who I know all of you are familiar with, is going to talk a little bit about the three of them. I know, sometimes we would like to ignore the elephant in the room, however, we can learn a great deal on how to keep that elephant from growing. Let's see what he has to say about what he has to offer our team.

Additional Resources

- Stephen Covey's *7 Habits of Highly Effective People* — His 7th Habit, Sharpening the Saw is a great reminder that we must continue to use our strengths if they are to serve us well.

- *The Imposter Cure: Escape the Mind-Trap of Imposter Syndrome* by Dr. Jessamy Hibberd.

The Elephant in the Room

Communication, Conflict, and Conversations

"People don't care how much you know until they know how much you care."

Theodore Roosevelt

Communicate. Communicate. Communicate. You hear about its importance all the time. It continues to be talked about, sometimes ad nauseam. It's like customer service. People can tell you what excellent customer service is and yet there continue to be workshops and books focused on the topic. Why? Because we are all still trying to get it right and learn not only how to deliver exemplary customer service but the most effective way to communicate.

My place on the team is to encourage you to communicate and give you a heads-up when a conversation needs to be held. Yep, you guessed it. I am the elephant in the room. I show up everywhere—in the workplace, with friends, in your head, at home. Wherever there are people, you can find me. I represent the topic you know needs to be addressed, yet for whatever reason you, and others, keep putting it off.

People avoid me like the plague, and yet I'm pretty popular because I come up in conversations all the time. They do their darndest to ignore me for as long as possible. I might begin small, but if left alone, I just get bigger and bigger and bigger until I'm so big that you can't ignore me any longer.

People feed me by leaving me alone and letting thoughts and stories fester in their heads. Other times, they feed me by talking with everyone except the person or people to whom they know they need to be talking. They know I'm there and there's a lot at stake, yet no one wants to talk about the issue until it's almost out of control.

The good news is that there isn't always only one way to communicate. There are, however, ways that can be more or less effective than others. Whether you're in the workplace or at home, I know you already understand the importance of communication. It's one of the top challenges in marriages, ranking right up there with money.

I get it. It's hard to talk about uncomfortable topics like money, projects, and change you don't agree with and yet you realize there's another way to do things, other than yours. It doesn't make one person or process necessarily right or wrong, better or worse. It just means you and the other person have a difference of opinion. We just need to decide to take the plunge and talk about them. Don't worry, we're going to check out some strategies for this at the end of the chapter. You get to decide what method works best for you.

So how do you know I'm in the room?

There are a variety of things I do to alert you.

I usually begin as the little voice in your head that puts you on notice and nudges you about a conversation which needs to happen either with yourself or others. No matter where or with whom, if I'm ignored, I keep growing and growing and growing. If you continue to ignore me, which often happens, I grow into an enormous, annoying trumpet blast that keeps yelling at you to talk about a topic or issue. Unfortunately, when I keep growing, so do the feelings of dread and anxiety over having the conversation. The entire conversation can be blown way out of proportion sometimes because of the stories you tell yourself in your head, which, many times, turn out not even to be true.

You might feel a knot or pit in your stomach, for one. People will most likely be talking about the topic behind closed doors, at the water cooler, or at happy hour. The problem is, it's rarely brought up with everyone who needs to discuss it. Sometimes the conversation happens in your head and your mind allows it to spiral out of control, many times without the facts. There may be silence in the room where you can hear a pin drop, or that uncomfortable silence where you wish someone would say something, but no one does.

Better yet, there's incessant chatter about nothing. You know people are trying to buy time, or should I say *run out of time*—too bad, so sad, we don't have time to address the issue. It will just have to wait until the next meeting. Well, you may not have eaten anything, but the elephant has—and he has just gotten bigger and bigger and bigger. No matter which it is, we know there's a topic no one wants to bring up, but everyone knows we need to address. It's always in the back or front of everyone's mind.

You should hear some of the stories people tell themselves about me! The stories may not be grounded in real life, just the reality in your own imagination. If I continue to be ignored, I can create and escalate conflicts. Whew!—I'm exhausted just thinking about it.

It's like you're walking on eggshells. Can you imagine me, an elephant, walking on eggshells? I'd break all of them no matter how hard or soft I stepped. If they weren't broken before, they will be now. If you don't address the elephant in the room, things will escalate and spiral out of control. Relationships may break. So let me do my job and lead you in knowing there's something you need to talk about. My nudge is delivered with compassion. Let me nudge you to have a conversation. The problem, many times, is because of a misunderstanding or miscommunication. If it is a difference of opinion, then talk about it and learn about the other person's point of view. The good news is if you hold the conversation, it is usually far less painful than the anticipation of addressing the issue.

In the book *Crucial Conversations*, the authors talk about the focus of stories. They discuss three conversations people have with themselves: the victim (poor us and look at all the things that have happened to us), the villain (those nasty people and what they have done to us—they are just plain bad and don't care about us), and the helpless (there's nothing more I can do or we blame others for the position in which we find ourselves).

It's a brilliant book and provides examples of crucial conversations and how to address them. Yes, things happen, but it's how we look at them and respond to them that makes or breaks the situation. I think overall people are good, they may make bad decisions or use poor judgment, but I don't think there are many people who get up in the morning and say, "I wonder how miserable I can make life for someone today."

I think most people want to have a good day and want others to have a good day too. As for the helpless, more people can help themselves and have resources to make the situation better. We can respect an opinion and still not agree with it. It's a choice.

It's a mystery to me why people avoid me. I know my size can be intimidating. My wrinkled, gray exterior is as tough as the conversations that need to be held and questions you know you need to ask. I know I said it's a mystery why I'm avoided, but you and I know it may not really be that much of a mystery.

People avoid tough conversations for lots of reasons. One of the most common ones I hear is that of fear. Here's one thing I think you and I can agree on: if you ignore the conversation, peace and a resolution are rarely found. If you decide to engage in the conversation, it may or may not prevent conflict, but if you at least get things out in the open, you have a good chance to discover a solution and can move on.

In my experience, as shared with my team members, people avoid that conversation looming over them for some of the following reasons:

- Don't want to hurt anyone's feelings.
- Aren't sure how to approach the person or subject.
- Feel as if they don't have the time to invest in the conversation.
- Fear of their own ego or feelings being hurt.
- Don't want people to be angry with them.
- Not confident in the knowledge they have coming into the conversation.
- Unsure of how to begin the conversation.
- Fear of retribution.

- Fear of losing a job, friendship, respect.
- Fear of becoming too emotional.
- The complexity and significance of the topic.
- Don't want the challenge(s) the conversation may bring.
- Detest conflict (any kind of conflict).
- Concerned the outcome may not be in their favor.
- Fear of the unknown.
- Tired of addressing the same topic over and over.

Wow, no wonder I'm in so many rooms. I might avoid myself, too. Just kidding!

When talking to and with herself and others, Ann works to remember the acronym she learned from Peter, a master coach and her instructor, during her coaching education. It serves her well in listening to others and when the parrot shows up with her self-talk—W.A.I.T.—Why Am I Talking? She also added an S to the acronym. W.A.I.S.T.—Why Am I Still Talking? This has served her well in the workplace and in her personal life, most especially with her son. How she wished she had done more of this when he was little.

Arlene and Ann: Conflict and the Conversation

Years ago, Arlene, one of Ann's long-time friends, and Ann, both volunteered and served on the same Regional Board of Directors for the Region 7 Jaycees (a group of approximately 30 chapters in Central Iowa). They shared the same vision and goal. They just had very different approaches to communicating and working on achieving it. Ann led the Board as Regional Director and Arlene was one of the seven District Directors.

The grapevine shared with Ann that Arlene referred to her as *"she."* Each time they were together, whether it was just the two of them or in a group of people, I could feel the tension grow. They did a great job of feeding me. Then, one cold and snowy December night, they were supposed to visit the Creston chapter, about 90 miles one way. Traveling together in Ann's car, they headed to Creston, Iowa. The temperature on the inside of the car was colder than on the outside, and it was below freezing out there.

You may be thinking, *why in the world were those two riding in the same car?* Looking back, I asked myself that same question. However, it was more economical, and I'd like to say safer. Then, the snow began to fall. Moving from being able to see miles in front of them with a clear vision to nearly blinding conditions in a few quick minutes, they determined it would be safer to turn around and go back home. Sometimes, the first step in mending a relationship or starting a conversation is finding common ground. Both agreed, turning around was the right decision. Shocked by this, I began to listen, and they began to talk.

At first the conversation consisted of random small talk. Nothing controversial. Nothing heavy. The weather, the radio, things that you couldn't fight over. The longer they talked, the more the conversation drifted to bigger, more important things in life. They talked about their values, growing up, hopes, dreams, and fears. Two and a half hours later, still sitting in the car with the engine running and the heat on, they began talking about their relationship with the volunteers and the Board. Each listened and slowly let down their guard.

The proverbial ice began to melt within each of them. Once they reached the actual issue, the way they were working toward their goal of being recognized as the number one region in America, and talked about it, they had a deeper understanding of where each was coming from. Ironically, they agreed on many things and had the best interest of the volunteers and board at heart. They still didn't necessarily agree 100 percent with each other or about how they worked, yet they had a newly discovered respect for each other.

I think they both finally felt heard. Like Garrison Wynn said, "No communication takes place until the other person feels heard."

Oh, by the way, you might be thinking why didn't Ann invite Arlene into her house instead of talking in the car. How rude? I wondered about that too, and so did she when she looked back on the conversation. Yet, had Ann invited Arlene into her house, a pause in the conversation would have occurred, and the entire conversation may have never unfolded as it did. Sometimes, things happen exactly as they're meant to.

Fast forward—their Board and entire region enjoyed being recognized as the number one region in America that year, not because of one person, one Board, or one year's worth of work, but because of the vision and tireless efforts of all volunteers who served that year, as well as all of whom worked countless hours and years before them, setting them up for success.

To this day, Ann and Arlene are still great friends.

Students and Feedback

When Ann was teaching a class years ago, one of her students made this comment when she was returning the draft of her team's research paper, "Oh, no. It looks like there's a lot of red on the paper."

Ann, glad to have heard her comment, shared with her that her job was to help her team learn as much as possible. By providing constructive comments, they could learn what it takes to write a more formal paper and ask more thought-provoking questions now and in the future. Accepting or rejecting the comments was totally up to the authors of the papers. She wanted to give them cause to pause and ask themselves which approach was more effective. It wasn't about her. It was about the courage to communicate with them in a positive manner, supporting them in staying curious, and developing their critical-thinking skills. The elephant would have grown had she not addressed the comment.

"In many ways, effective communication begins with mutual respect, communication that inspires, encourages others to do their best."

Zig Ziglar

Lessons Learned

- Have the conversation, even when it is difficult and even when you don't feel like it (Lynn).

- When most people hear the word conflict, they get a sick feeling in their stomach. I know some conflict can be challenging and even negative; however, conflict, when handled well, can be very productive. Many leaders don't want people to always agree with them. They welcome healthy conversations with questions, which will strengthen the company. In our personal lives, these conversations can enhance our relationships.

- Bottom line, talk about what's on our minds and bothering us, because if we don't it's just going to escalate and keep getting bigger and bigger. That baby elephant doesn't stay little for very long! If we talk about the issue, we have a good chance of moving the conversation forward, solving the problem, and strengthening the relationship.

- Discuss boundaries.

- The thought of having a conversation and talking about a topic is usually worse than the actual conversation.

- By starting with the little things early in life, we can help the younger members of society learn to ponder the bigger questions. Recognize that something seemingly small to an adult could be a big deal to a child. To them, not being asked to play a game or be part of a team is a big deal.

- If we give people the chance to share how they feel and what they're thinking, not only do we have a deeper understanding of where they're coming from, they also know we really care what they think, and the relationship is richer because of it.

- It takes courage to talk about the hard things.

- Conflict doesn't have to be negative. It can be positive. It's good news you and our team have differing opinions, ideas, and ways of accomplishing things. Because of your differences, chances are you'll find the best way to move forward. In the end, does it matter who came up with the idea as long as it's what's best for all involved? Besides, if we all cheered for the same team, think how boring Super Bowl parties might be!

- The quote, "People don't care how much you know, until they know how much you care," really holds true. We just need to remember to incorporate it into our daily habits.

- In the end you can always, after weighing the pros and cons, decide it's not the right time for the conversation. Maybe there's someone else who can be more effective in sharing the information, or the conversation isn't necessary.

My Strength

- Letting you know there's a conversation needed and an issue to be addressed.

Your Strengths (List the strengths you see in yourself when it comes to communication, conflict, and conversations.)

Strategies: Choose the one(s) which will best serve you.

- Find a safe and neutral space to talk about the issue. Don't have the conversation in someone's office if you can help it. The reason? The person whose office you are in subconsciously has more control than the other person, even if not intentional. It's a subconscious feeling. On a side note, if you have a tough topic to discuss with your teens, especially with boys, talk in the car. It's easier to talk if you don't have to look at the person all the time. Eye contact is important, yet sometimes so is side-by-side when you're connecting with your sons.

- Get yourself in a good frame of mind.

- Ask yourself and the other person what outcome you both would like to see at the end of the conversation.

- What, if any, challenges do you anticipate during the conversation?

- Talk to each other.

- Listen to each other.

- Have a candid conversation with yourself about why the conversation is important to you.

- Use "I" statements. The word "you" puts people on the defensive more times than not.

- Consider what you are going to do or say to help the other person/people feel more comfortable in talking about me, "the elephant" in the room.

- Stick to the facts regarding the issue. They are true and indisputable.

- Remember, opinions are not right or wrong—it's the way you feel about an issue.

- Share your feelings and take ownership of them. In other words, others don't necessarily "make you mad." We allow ourselves to become angry. Wait until you're in the right frame of mind and rational. If addressing an issue when you're really hurt or angry it's easy to say things you don't really mean and use a voice that comes across as loud and obnoxious, or not as clear or kind as you'd like it to.

- Step back, take time to think about things, and choose words carefully, while still staying true to yourself.

- Share what bothered you about the comment or situation.

- Seek first to understand, then work to be understood. Do you want to be understood? I'm guessing that's a big hell yes! Remember, so does the other person.

- Ask questions. Listen. Acknowledge what they said. Discuss. Repeat.

- Stick to the behavior. Don't attack the person.

- Ask the "W" questions without asking "why." *Why* puts people on the defensive. People feel as if you're questioning them, their knowledge, or decision. I know you're asking for understanding, but that's not always their perception. A person's perception is their reality—it's true in their world, just like our perceptions are true in our world. I like open-ended questions. I especially like questions beginning with "What." *What* opens doors and helps people know you want to know what they are thinking. You'll discover the why and reasons behind decisions and beliefs. You still don't have to agree with them. However, having a deeper understanding of where a person is coming from helps to create empathy. When you can empathize and share that you understand a person's feelings, you can create a common understanding and create trust.

- For Example: Would you rather have someone say, "Why did you buy that book or make that decision?" or "What inspired you to buy that book or make that decision?" You can also ask them to share more about the decision. Tell them you are interested in knowing more so you can support them or share with others depending on the circumstances.

- In the end you can always, after weighing the pros and cons, decide it's not the right time for the conversation, there's someone else who can be more effective in sharing the information, or the conversation isn't necessary.

- Talk deadlines. This will help eliminate confusion, conflict, and misunderstandings. Don't use the acronym ASAP. What does this really mean? I mean, I know we know it to mean *as soon as possible*, but does that mean Right Now! Or as soon as I can possibly get to it? Who's right? Both! So instead of ASAP, talk about deadlines like, "By when do we/you want/need to have something completed?" If you ask someone for a deadline and they won't give it to you, suggest a deadline. I'm certain they'll tell you if it doesn't fit with their schedule. Negotiate and work out a timeline together. Then follow it up in an email so you both have not only a record of it but to ensure both of you have the same understanding of the agreed-upon timeline. Something to watch out for—be sure you're specific, for example, don't say, "the end of the day," because your end of the day may differ from their end of the day. Be specific and say, "If I get it to you by 4:30 this afternoon, does that work for you?" They can say yes or no, but at least you both can talk it over and are clear.

Your Reflection

Reflection Questions: Answer here or in a separate journal.

1. What causes me to be/feel uncomfortable?
2. What's my elephant nudging me to bring up?
3. What elephants have I been avoiding or letting grow?
4. What am I going to do to address the elephant in the room?
5. What conversation do I need to have with myself?
6. What strategies am I going to try when addressing the elephant in the room?

Your biggest take-away(s) Regarding Communication, Conflict, and Conversations

Your Action Plan

Here is an example of what your action plan may look like. Remember it's your plan not mine, this is only an example to support you in getting started. Choose the action which will support you in moving forward. There is space for you to write your personal plan of action at the end of the example.

1. *Goal: To address challenging conversations even if it's uncomfortable.*

2. *Action: I will work hard to use facts in conversations as well as using the "I" statements more, especially when it comes to how I feel. I will also address conversations sooner rather than later. I may practice what I'm going to say so I say what I mean and am kind. I am going to use "What" instead of "Why" as much as possible when asking questions. I'm also going to reread the book, Crucial Conversations.*

3. *Who will support me? I can practice my conversations with my husband. If the conversation is going to be with my husband, Shelley can support me in talking over how to approach the conversation.*

4. *Date: Reread the book by December 31*

5. *How will I know I'm making progress? I will be cognizant of using the "I" statements and reduce the use of the word "you" because it puts people on the defensive. The conversation will remain civil and not turn into an argument but be more of a discussion where all parties are heard.*

Your Turn: Answer here or in a separate journal.

1. Goal:

2. Action:

3. Who can support you?

4. Date to begin:

5. How will you know you made progress?

While I want you to address the issues, the next member of the team will entice you to put things off for as long as possible. Let's see how the monkey on our back, while challenging, can still serve us well.

Additional Resources

- *Crucial Conversations* by Patterson, Grenny, McMillan and Switzler.

- *Conversational Intelligence* by Judith Blaser.

- *Conversation Gardens: Where Conversations Flow and Relationships Grow* by Lynn Kuhn.

- *The Advice Monster* by Michael Bungay Stanier.

- *The Seven Habits of Highly Successful People* by Stephen Covey.

- *Leadership: Coaching with a Growth Mindset* by Simon Sinek (TEDx).

- *Why There's So Much Conflict at Work and What You Can Do To Fix It* by Liz Kislik (TEDx).

The Monkey on Your Back

Procrastination

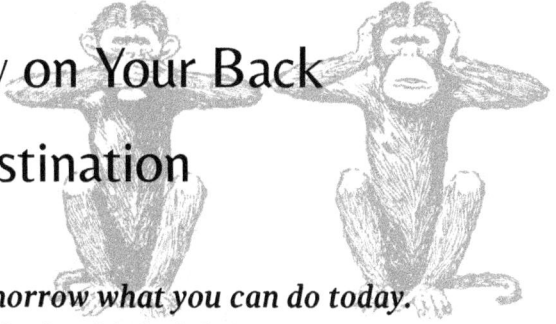

"My advice is never do tomorrow what you can do today. Procrastination is the thief of time."

Charles Dickens and David Copperfield

hen I first met the geese, I knew we had a lot to talk about, and yet all I really wanted to do was wait and do it tomorrow. Oh, the art of procrastination: my specialty!

Can you relate? Do you ever put things off when you know they need to be done, but for some reason you are just not into doing it? The geese do a good job of knowing that no matter what we bring to the table or are struggling with, there is value somewhere to be found. They help you manage it. However, they also make sure everyone knows they need to pull their weight on the team. I might be able to ride on someone's back for a short time, but can't make a habit of it. If you don't address the project or conversation, that sick uneasy and stressed feeling is there consciously or subconsciously.

I'm the one that's constantly on your mind, nagging you about that project you've been putting off. You can't always see me, but you know I'm there. Every. Single. Minute. You guessed it. I'm the monkey on your back. I met a famous manager in another book, *The One Minute Manager Meets the Monkey* by Hal Burrows, Ken Blanchard, and William Oncken. It's a great read.

Most people don't like to procrastinate let alone want to admit they procrastinate. Yet most people do it at one time or another. I wonder why people procrastinate because I know it causes them stress, sometimes more stress than people care to admit. I bet when you procrastinate, you are stressed. Ann is. It can even cause analysis paralysis. Mitch Matthews suggests procrastination may be part of perfectionism. With all this you may wonder what value I could possibly bring since I'm somewhat annoying.

Well, I keep whatever you need to do top of mind. My little voice is always there, lurking around in your thoughts. I encourage you to examine the reason you procrastinate and to ask yourself, do you have a good reason to put off doing something or are you finding excuses? No matter the reason or excuse, it's a good idea to examine the "why" behind your own procrastination. No judgment because you can't change what you don't acknowledge, so we may as well talk about it before it becomes even bigger than my friend, the elephant in the room. The trick is figuring out the reason we procrastinate, finding the courage to talk about it, and then figuring out how we are going to manage it.

I'm going to focus on the projects, since the elephant on this team focuses on conversations. For example, there's something that needs your attention. Maybe it's a paper that needs to be written, a system needing to be developed or updated, or a project that needs to be completed. It might be a self-imposed project, such as a home project, a book to write, or a resume to update. No matter what the environment or circumstance, you know something needs to be completed. So why do you ignore it and put it off? Do you think if you ignore it long enough, it will just get tired and go away?

Wrong!

The longer you ignore and put off doing whatever it is which needs to be done, the heavier and more annoying I become. Stress and anxiety continue to build, especially when a deadline looms. When people wait until the last minute to finish whatever it is they've ignored, several outcomes are possible: a deadline may be missed, the quality of the project may be compromised, stress is heightened, jobs or even people's health are in jeopardy.

The biggest problem is that if things turn out well, you may never have a reason to stop waiting until the last minute to finish things. You'll keep procrastinating, experiencing stress until you miss a deadline or finally decide you can't take it anymore and resolve to get to work and change your habits.

In her many years of teaching, Ann discovered that I'm quite popular on college campuses. Students procrastinate. They love monkeys! Don't get me wrong, not all students procrastinate, yet many do. They put off doing homework, asking questions about assignments they don't understand, or even working with their team until the last minute. I ask myself why students do this. I don't understand it, yet many of them do it. All. The. Time.

I'm sure part of the challenge for her students and most people is they know all the things they want to do to get to where they want to be. However, sometimes looking at all those tasks they think, "How am I ever going to get it all done?" So sometimes when you let yourself get overwhelmed, you do nothing or everything except what you're supposed to be or need to be doing. For example, do you sleep too much, play video games, do laundry, clean, play on social media?

The list can go on and on. All it does is delay the inevitable, which means you're stressed and upset when you go to work on the project and are up against a deadline and feel the time crunch. You do the best they can, kind of, but is it your best work? Are you stressed that it could have been better if you had just begun earlier?

Putting things off happens to everyone.

My place on the team is secure.

Based on my observations and conversations, I've discovered some of the following reasons—which is not to say *all* the reasons—that exist.

- You're overwhelmed.
- Just plain don't like and don't want to work on the project.
- The task or project is boring or seems irrelevant.
- There are a million other things you want to do instead of what needs to be done.
- Adrenaline rush. Some people thrive on the last-minute adrenaline rush with the mounting pressure of finishing it just in time.
- You're depressed.
- You're not in the mood to do it.
- You don't know how to do something.
- You don't want to ask for help (when in reality, people will help you if you ask).
- It's not really that important to you. However, it's important to differentiate between a project at work or home that has to be done or a project of your own choosing. If it's your own project and you're procrastinating, maybe it's time to ask yourself how important is this to me.

- Fear—not being sure of what exactly you are supposed to be doing, wondering if you know enough to complete the task, are good enough, or if your product/service will meet expectations (yours or someone else's), the unknown, being judged or criticized by others or yourself, wondering if the end product will be good enough, will you fail or succeed?

Can you relate to any of the reasons above?

Ann and the Avoiding the Budget Narrative

When Ann worked at the American Cancer Society, she wrote a grant with her friends, Carol and Carlyn, from the American Lung Association and the American Heart Association. In charge of writing the budget and budget narrative, among other sections, Ann delayed completing and writing the final copy until the night before it was due. Why she was assigned to write the budget and its narrative, she will never know. It was not her strongest talent or interest.

She worked on it during the weeks leading up to the deadline, yet never quite finished it. Then crunch time hit and it took an all-nighter to finish it. Looking back, I wonder if she put off doing the budget section because she didn't want to do it, didn't have time with all the other projects, wasn't sure what the heck she was doing, or was fearful of not having it be good enough. Truth be told, it might have been a combination of all the above!

Walking into the office the next morning, her supervisor asked her what time she went to bed. Her response—"I haven't yet."

I'm happy to report at 4 o'clock that afternoon, after meeting with her grant partners and hitting send to the Robert

Wood Johnson Foundation, she went home and went to bed. Several months later, after the Foundation reviewers read all submissions and completed their site visits, including a visit to Iowa, the team received word they had been awarded the grant. Much to their delight, the coalition and state of Iowa received over $1 million dollars to invest and implement the tobacco prevention and educational programs requested. That was over two decades ago, and the memory remains. What did she learn? It's better to begin early, make significant progress, and ask for help if and when you need it.

Ann and This Book — Procrastination at its Finest

This book is another good example of Ann procrastinating, though since you're reading it, she overcame the obstacles surrounding it. I've been hanging out with Ann and a book for quite a while. She dreamed and talked about writing a book for years, decades, to be perfectly honest. Yet it's only been in the last three or four years that she said it out loud and shared it with friends.

But she didn't start it right away. I just kept hanging out on her back, nagging her, getting heavier each day, and wondering when she was going to write and finish this first book. I kept asking her, "Are you going to do this or not?"

Granted, the book was a self-inflicted monkey on her back because no one except herself was pressuring her to write it. A couple of trusted and caring friends asked her why writing a book was important to her. They even said it was okay to decide not to write the book if it wasn't a goal anymore. Now, that was tough to think about and hear, but necessary all the same. When she saw others accomplishing what she said she wanted to do, she had a heart-to-heart conversation with herself and asked a couple of tough questions. By the way, don't ask yourself or others questions you don't really want to know the answer to.

The questions were, "Why do I keep putting off writing a book? Why do I want to write a book? Was writing a book still important to me?" She tried to practice what she preached and ask the questions with kindness and compassion. It's easy for her to ask other people questions and show kindness and compassion, but for herself, not so much. I bet you can relate. You're probably harder on yourself than anyone else. Or are your own best or worst critic depending on how you look at it? Alas, that parrot continues to show up like the rest of us.

So, in writing this first book, were there excuses or genuine reasons it took so long? Honestly, there were both. Here are some questions Ann asked herself and the answers she discovered. Even though they're about this book, you can substitute your own projects when you ask yourself questions about the reasons you procrastinate.

Here are some excerpts from Ann's conversations with herself and trusted friends.

Is writing a book important? Yes.

Why is writing a book important? I truly want to share things that I've learned along life's path, support people in accomplishing their goals, and make a difference in someone's life. If I could make a difference in one person's life through sharing my experiences or inspire and empower people to believe in themselves and appreciate what they brought to the world, that would be enough for me. I've also shared with Noah to go after your dreams and have fun doing it. I want to be an excellent role model and set a good example for Noah.

Is fear playing a role in procrastinating? That's a *big* hell yes! What if people didn't like it? But as several people shared, what if they do like it? What if others can relate to the same challenges I have? What if together, we can overcome fear and learn how to work with our internal team and lead ourselves to success? My friends shared; no one will like it or hate it unless you write it, so they can read it.

Do I have the knowledge needed to write a book and publish it? Yes and no. I had an idea of what to do and on what I wanted to focus. But did I know how to publish it? Heck no. Finally asking for help and finding the right resources were the best things that I did to support myself on the journey. Thank you, Self-Publishing School (now Self-Publishing) team, Coach Kerk, my family and my friends. Because of you, I didn't have to do all of this on my own!

Do I have time, and do I commit to things so I can use the excuse I didn't have time? Yes. And No. I like to volunteer and be involved with the community. When you like to be involved with things and volunteer, which is important to me, it's hard to say no. However, there is the danger of over-committing. I had to remember that just because I said no, it didn't mean no forever, it just meant not right now. Eventually, I realized it was time to either write the book or let it go. I started saying no to things I wanted to do (not no forever, just no, for now) so I could make time and honor a goal important to me.

See how easy it is to go down the rabbit hole with all these questions? What's important is to unpack and answer the questions one at a time!

So, there you have it—transparency into Ann's thoughts.

Bottom line: Ann had to figure out why she procrastinated in working on something she said was important. She was lucky to have friends who were also writing books and were in varying stages of the process. Each inspired her in different ways. Some were already published authors, some in the editing and formatting stage, others in the rough-draft stages, and others were outlining and mind mapping. A few were still in the idea stage. Like the geese, all were headed in the same direction, publishing their book, and when one was tired there was always someone to take the lead, providing support for the other as long as it was needed.

Lessons Learned

- Being busy and productive are not synonymous. I can help you procrastinate by keeping you busy, but this stops you from being productive. If you put things off, there are consequences like stress, loss of sleep, and loss of time worrying about things.

- Many times, the anticipation of working on whatever it is you're putting off doing is far worse than actually doing the work or having the conversation.

- Self-awareness is the first step. You can change what you acknowledge. There will always be monkeys on your back. The question is how many at one time, and how will you choose to manage them?

- Most of us still procrastinate on something. Here's a question that will help you figure out why you're procrastinating! Is what you're doing as important to you as you say it is? Ann's friend, Lynn, shares in her book, *Conversation Gardens: Where Conversations Flow and Relationships Grow*, three types of "cranstinations!"

1. Pre-crastination—those that work on a project early and actually create more work for themselves because they didn't take the time to think, research, and plan for what was needed for the project.

2. Plan-crasination—the idea of stopping and planning, making a list, and prioritizing what needs to be done and yet not really getting started.

3. Procrastination—the art of putting things off until the last minute or forever.

My Strengths

- I bring a project to your attention and continue to bring the project to your attention to the point of being annoying.

- I encourage you to ask yourself tough questions and figure out the reason for procrastinating.

Your Strengths (List the strengths you see in yourself when it comes to overcoming procrastination.)

Strategies: Choose the one(s) which will best serve you.

- Ask yourself the tough questions when you find yourself procrastinating. By the way, are there reasons and excuses when procrastinating? Absolutely. The challenge is in having the courage to figure out if you are making excuses or if there are legitimate reasons. No matter why you're procrastinating, address it, figure out what to do about it, then take action. Answering the following questions can help get you "unstuck."
  - What am I getting by procrastinating?
  - Am I putting it off because it's hard?

- What's the worst thing that can happen and can I prevent it from happening?

- If the worst thing happens, what will I do?

- What are the biggest obstacles in completing this project?

- How can I overcome the obstacles in my way?

- Do I delay doing the same things repeatedly?

- In what way(s) is this project or activity relevant? You may have to ask what is relevant to what? For example: Someone may be tired of school and yet they know that to have the opportunities and salary they want in their chosen field, it's important to attend and finish grad school. Or maybe it's a project the organization wants you to complete, and your part will support the organization in achieving its goal, which ultimately helps with profitability and job security.

- How do I feel when I procrastinate?

- Ask for help—people are happy to be there to support you, whether it's cheering you on, helping you learn how to do whatever it is you need to learn, or working alongside you.

- Balance your time. If you have to write a paper or whatever, work on it and decide on some type of reward when you're finished. Work a while, do something fun. Get up early to get it done so you can have fun later.

- Use procrastination as a tool—don't let it use you (Aree).

- Hire a coach.

- Work with a trusted friend.

- Make a decision to stop procrastinating and write your plan.

- Consciously change your mindset. For example, if you don't like to exercise (which Ann doesn't) reframe your thinking and think of it as increasing your activity. If you're an entrepreneur and are uncomfortable marketing yourself, think about it as sharing what you have to offer.

- Set deadlines. Adjust if needed. Refrain from using the acronym ASAP. Yes, it means as soon as possible, but does that mean—Right Now! Or as soon as I can possibly get to it? Who's right? Both! So, talk about deadlines. When do you need to have something completed? If you ask someone for a deadline and they won't give it to you, suggest a deadline. If it doesn't fit with their schedule, negotiate a timeline together. Follow it up in an email so you both have a record of it and ensure each has the same understanding of the agreed upon timeline.

- Use a calendar—block time to work on or complete the project and honor your time.

- **TIVO** is your friend. Watching TV or a favorite movie is one of Ann's distractions. She asks herself after spending an hour or more watching TV, "why did I watch that when I could have been working on my goal?" TIVO your favorite shows. Ann loves *The Voice, Law and Order*, game shows, and, of course, the Christmas Movies on the *Hallmark Channel*. Her husband laughs with her, well probably at her, but that's okay. He reminds her there's a love story, a problem, and a happy ending as all the movies work out in the end. She continues to share that while this is true, she believes people enjoy a happy ending and it gives people hope and belief in the good of society.

Bottom line, I'm going to continue to be annoying, invade your thoughts, and hang out until you decide what to do to take care of me. You can either start or finish the project or address the issue(s) that are challenging you and begin new habits to reduce procrastinating.

Your Reflection

Reflection Questions: Answer here or in a separate journal. **— By the way please don't keep putting off writing your reflection or determining your action plan. I'm kidding. It's your journey.**

1. What are the actual reasons I procrastinate or delay moving forward? Be honest with yourself. Remember, no judgment.

2. Am I putting this off because it's hard? I don't want to do it? I don't like to do it?

3. What do I get/gain from procrastinating?

4. What are the strategies which most appeal to me?

5. How can I overcome the obstacles standing in my way so that I stop or reduce the number of times I procrastinate?

Your Biggest Take-away(s) Regarding Procrastination

Your Action Plan

Here is an example of what your action plan may look like. Remember it's your plan not mine, this is only an example to support you in getting started. Choose the action which will support you in moving forward. There is space for you to write your personal plan of action at the end of the example.

1. Goal: Finish projects at least one day before they are due so I'm not stressed at the last minute.

2. Action: Take time, and be honest with myself, to ask myself the real reason I am procrastinating and what I am getting out of waiting until the last minute. I also know this is easier said than done. I will ask for help if I don't know how to do something. I will put projects and action steps on the calendar, stick to the timeline, and make myself work on the hardest activities when I'm at my best, which is first thing in the morning. Then I will celebrate the progress made.

3. Who will support me? My husband or peer depending on the project.

4. Date: Today and each time I put off doing something.

5. How will I know I'm making progress? I will be finished with the project at least one day before it is due and not feel as stressed.

Your Turn: Answer here or in a separate journal.

1. Goal:
2. Action:
3. Who can support you?
4. Date to begin:
5. How will you know you made progress?

Now that we have some insight as to why procrastination shows up and how to work with it, let's see how the ostrich can help us focus on issues instead of avoiding them.

Additional Resources

- *Every Entrepreneur Needs Systems for Mindset* by Kelly Azevedo.

- *Conversation Gardens: Where Conversations Flow and Relationships Grow* by Lynn Kuhn.

- Mitch Matthews—podcast—Encourage the Encourager # 003 Procrastination or Perfectionism.

- *The One Minute Manager* by <u>Ken Blanchard</u> and <u>Spencer Johnson</u>.

- *The One Minute Manager Meets the Monkey* by Hal Burrows, Ken Blanchard, and William Oncken.

- *The Psychology of Procrastination: Understand Your Habits, Find Motivation, and Get Things Done* by Hayden Finch, PhD.

- *The Confidence Code* by Deaon McGhee.

The Ostrich

Avoiding or Focusing

*"Lack of direction, not lack of time, is the problem.
We all have twenty-four-hour days."*

Zig Ziglar

Do you ever hear people saying, "Go ahead. Put your head in the sand!"

I bet you already have a picture of me, the ostrich, with my head in the sand. You may be laughing or thinking, "Yeah, I can relate to this statement." Ann can. Sometimes people do this to avoid something because they just don't have the time, energy, or interest to face it at the moment.

When this phrase is used, people think I'm oblivious to things or trying to avoid my surroundings or a conflict, which admittedly at times, maybe I am.

I suppose it could be said there are times it's good to have your head in the sand, for if you thought about all the things going on you might never accomplish anything. By blocking out certain things, it may give you ample space to consider the reasons a subject is bothersome. You might lose focus because of that darn squirrel in your head. Granted, if you keep your head in the sand and ignore the situation for too long, you may find the elephant entering the room, or the monkey climbing on your back. Don't worry, it's not all doom and gloom!

I challenge you to look at me from another perspective—the other side of what that statement could mean is this; when I have my head in the sand, I may be working to focus on something specific.

How do you know when you're putting your head in the sand to focus or ignore the pending unpleasant task or conversation?

My friends and I have found that when people have a pit in their stomach, a little nagging voice in their head, or my friend the monkey on their back, it's easy to put their head in the sand and pretend the situation will just go away. As the elephant and monkey know, it doesn't just go away. Maybe it does for the time being, but before long it will surface again, and usually it will be even bigger. We are all challenged or afraid at one time or another of what we might find and learn. Blocking things out and not thinking of them brings peace in the moment. However, in the long run, avoiding the issue or task fuels my friends the monkey or the elephant far too long and we all know where they end up—on your back or taking over the room.

I can help you realize there is an issue that needs addressing and focus. If you feel like you have your head in the sand, ask yourself, *Why am I avoiding the issue?* Sometimes the things people avoid are conversations or projects they don't want to have or do for a variety of reasons. Other times, you may avoid things because you're tired of dealing with the same thing over and over again. Many times, my friends and I have found that thinking about it or the anticipation of doing something is far worse than addressing the topic head on or tackling the task.

It's good to acknowledge what could happen and prepare for it. Hope for the best, and then prepare for the worst. Ask yourself the "what if" questions. What if *blank* happens? Or what if it doesn't work out or what if I'm not chosen for a position? It's no wonder people put their heads in the sand and give me a bad rap. Well, what if *blank* happens or you aren't chosen? Is it the end of the world? It may feel like it is for a period of time but in all reality, not everything works out like we want it to. Disappointment helps you appreciate the good times and successes in life. I propose it's only a failure or mistake if we fail to learn from it.

As far as focusing and removing distractions, that can be challenging depending on where and what the distractions are. At work, the distractions can be many. Work locations look much different today than they did prior to the pandemic (COVID-19). The landscape of the work environment has changed. The "norm," which used to be going to the office on a daily basis has drastically changed since the pandemic. Some things for the good, some maybe not.

Distractions at the "old" office were peers stopping by to talk, emails, phone calls, meetings. Today, distractions at the "new" office at home are emails, zoom meeting fatigue, lack of human face-to-face interactions, laundry, pets, kiddos, dishes. You get the picture.

Can you do two things at once and do them well? Yes, maybe, and probably not.

Can you watch TV and write at the same time? Can you work on two books at the same time? Depends on how much time and attention you want and need to give to each project. Depending on the intensity of the project, if most are honest, people seem to be more productive and successful putting their head in the sand and focusing on one thing at a time. That does not mean you have to finish everything before you work on a different project, because let's face it, most people have multiple projects going on at the same time. However, when you're focused and reduce the distractions, you can make more significant progress on whatever project you're working on at the moment.

Ann has a couple of books she wants to write and when she was writing this book, she got stuck. She realized when working on the book she needed to close all files except the ones for this book so she could focus. One of the best tips she discovered was to put all book files on a thumbdrive. This way she can work on her book on the computer in her office, or her laptop at the kitchen table, on the patio, or in a coffee shop. She can plug it into her laptop and not have to worry about where the files are or which file is the most up-to-date document. Sounds easy, yet sometimes the obvious, like the trees in the forest, are right in front of us, yet we are blind to them. Listening to music is inspiring, yet when it came to the final edit of the book, the music had to be turned off so she could focus on what to write to get it right for you, the reader.

Ann has put her head in the sand for both reasons, to avoid things and to focus on them. Putting her head in the sand to avoid things doesn't happen as much as it used to, mainly because she's aware of it and is working to address things at the right time. It doesn't mean she's successful all the time, but she keeps trying like everyone else. Now, more times than not, when she puts her head in the sand it's usually to focus. She works to create space to concentrate on the issue(s) she's been avoiding as well as the tasks at hand, whether it's faith, family, work, writing, reading, scrapbooking, or making plans for her podcast. Eliminating some of her distractions for at least the time being means gaining time to focus, figuring out how to proceed and being more productive.

"I don't care how much power, brilliance or energy you have, if you don't harness it and focus it on a specific target and hold it there, you're never going to accomplish as much as your ability warrants."

Zig Ziglar

Ann Learns from Her Clients

Some of Ann's clients are working to put their heads in the sand to focus and others to avoid topics. One client shared that she had so many interruptions, which in reality were her job, she had a hard time focusing on the big projects. Her daily routine remained the same, which didn't help in accomplishing her goals. She decided she would focus on her most challenging projects in the morning for an hour or two right after she checked her email. Besides working in the morning, she set her "out of the office" response and closed her door, sharing with her peers that if there was an emergency, she could still be reached. Another client decided to focus on writing reports in the morning and schedule meetings (the ones he could) during the afternoon, because meetings were easier to participate in than writing, and by the afternoon it took longer to write than in the morning when he was fresh.

Ann learned from working with several clients on this challenge that she may want to examine her schedule, too. She usually scheduled meetings in the morning, thinking *let's meet* and then she will work on the big projects, writing, and follow-up in the afternoon. She discovered she needed to work on writing and projects requiring more brain power in the mornings. Focusing or "putting her head in the sand" in the morning worked. Check email. Follow up on what must be done. Stay off social media for a set amount of time and set a timer for how long she would commit to working on a particular project. She also likes rewards, so there is usually a reward when achieving different benchmarks or milestones in a project. It might be a quick walk, working on a puzzle that night, or taking a break to talk to a peer. She could ignore the challenge of being more productive, or address it and make a change. Change can be good.

Ann, Doug, Noah, and the Football Game.

When Noah was around seven, Ann and Doug were at a football game. Her husband sat down upon returning from the concession stand. She thought she'd share with him her observation of Noah and Joel, one of his friends. They were yelling at the cute girls, "You're hot!" The girls just grinned, laughed, and kept walking. Note: his friend Joel has three older brothers. The girls knew him because they were friends of one of the brothers and were used to him giving them grief. Her husband laughed and said, "Yeah right. They're yelling, 'Go Hawks!'" (One of the local teams.)

She remembers saying, "Go ahead. Put your head in the sand. You think they're too young to be saying that, but I know what I heard them say."

A few minutes later, lo and behold, the boys were leaning over the guardrail and yelling, "You're hot!"

Doug's head whipped around and exclaimed, "Oh my God. You're right."

She laughed and blurted out, "Told ya." Not that she's a "told you so" kind of girl, because usually she isn't, but at that moment the shoe fit. They both laughed and listened even more attentively from that point forward.

Ann and Her New Supervisor

Assigned a new supervisor after a reorganization, Ann knew, based on experience with this person, the match may or may not work. She tried to be optimistic because she thought she could work with anyone. I'm uncertain if she had her head in the sand or was just trying to keep an open mind. Their styles, his dominant and egotistical demeanor and her accommodating and people pleasing, were like oil and water. Neither style better or worse, right or wrong, they were just extremely different.

Staffing a volunteer committee meeting together, her supervisor in charge, Ann, as a partner (to support him); he and the Volunteer Chair arrived just as the meeting was about to begin. Unfortunately, and quite obvious to her, they had stopped at a happy hour prior to the meeting. Ann had a couple of choices.

1. It would have been easy, well maybe not easy, to put her head in the sand, ignore the situation, and let him run the meeting with the possibility of embarrassing himself and the organization.

2. She could call him out on it and risk ruining an already strained relationship.

3. She could put her head in the sand to focus on what was best for the organization and offer to facilitate the meeting.

Knowing his position in the organization and pending retirement within a couple of years, she thought it best to offer to facilitate the meeting and not bring attention to the issue. Because of his position, it was better to ask not tell. She asked if he would like her to facilitate the meeting so he could focus on listening to the discussion and volunteers. He took her up on her offer. She facilitated the meeting, shared the incident with her former supervisor, and moved on. Looking back, she's glad she didn't avoid it or make a big scene.

Ann used to say in any given situation, "I would do..." It's easy to say I know what I'd do; however, she has learned over time and sometimes the hard way, you really don't know what you'd do unless you're in that position. Now she works to remember to say, "This is what I think I would do," or "this is what I hope I would do."

> *"Instead of focusing on those circumstances that you cannot change—focus strongly and powerfully on the circumstances that you can."*
>
> *Joy Page*

Lessons Learned

- Avoid or focus—you have your own unique perception of any given situation. It's all about how you look at things.

- It's about being honest with yourself by asking whether you are avoiding or focusing on something when and if you put your head in the sand.

- It's far better to figure out why we may be avoiding the issue and find time to focus on the challenge rather than to let it get bigger and bigger and become like my friend, the elephant in the room.

- Finding time to focus on the tasks will help you find peace of mind in your personal and professional life.

- You can either ignore issues or face them and figure out how to address them so you can be more productive. Because, as you well know, ignoring things doesn't mean they are going away.

My Strengths

- I help you focus and block the noise inside your head or that which surrounds you and gets in your way of working on what is most important.

- I support you in working on one thing at a time.

Your Strengths (List the strengths you see in yourself when it comes to focusing as opposed to avoiding things.)

Strategies: Choose the one(s) which will best serve you.

- Create space so you can focus on what you need to at the moment.

- Create a "parking lot" at home and work—a place to list ideas and projects you want to remember, just not this minute, so you can focus on the ones you need to in the moment. Once on the list, it's a relief not to have to remember it because everybody has so much on their mind it's impossible to remember everything there is to do. It can be on a flip chart at meetings, or for personal projects on a calendar, on paper or on your phone for future use.

- Ask yourself tough questions. For example, are you avoiding or focusing on the issue and why?

- Remove the distractions so you can focus on what's most important at the time (can change daily, monthly, and depending what season of life you find yourself in).
  - Put your phone away.
  - Silence your phone.
  - Turn off the TV.
  - Turn off notifications.
  - Turn off social media.
  - Turn off the music. (Never before have "turn offs" been more important.)
- Choose one major project to work on at a time (if possible).
- Address the situation. Get help if you need it. Learn from it. Move on.
- Use a calendar to stay organized.
- Journal.

Your Reflection

Reflection Questions: Answer here or in a separate journal.

1. When have I had "my head in the sand?" Has it been to avoid something, and I just haven't had the time, interest, or energy to face it, or has it been to focus?

2. Does someone else control my distractions? (Setting meetings, etc.)

3. On what am I focused or on what do I want to focus?

4. What helps keep me focused?

Your Biggest Take-away(s) Regarding Avoiding and Focusing

Your Action Plan

Here is an example of what your action plan may look like. Remember it's your plan not mine, this is only an example to support you in getting started. Choose the action which will support you in moving forward. There is space for you to write your personal plan of action at the end of the example.

1. *Goal: Stop interrupting myself and focus on one project at a time.*

2. *Action: Make a plan and put it in the calendar. Schedule time to check email, follow up, work on a specific project, return phone calls, and turn off notifications if possible. Limit my time on social media and not check my phone every few minutes. Set a timer for 30 minutes to work on a project and then assess where I am at the end of 30 minutes. At mealtime or when working on certain projects (writing ones for me) establish a phone-free zone. I will also set up a document so if an idea or a task pops into my head during a project I can write it where I will remember it and then get back to work immediately.*

3. *Who will support me? This one's on me during the day. During meals, my family can support me.*

4. *Date: Today*

5. *How will I know I'm making progress? I will be more productive and get things done in a more timely manner. I will have a "parking lot" document to record ideas and tasks. I will have a plan in my calendar for when I'm working on specific projects or tasks.*

Your Turn: Answer here or in a separate journal.

1. Goal:

2. Action:

3. Who can support you?

4. Date to begin:

5. How will you know you made progress?

It's hard to figure out whether or not you're focusing on something or avoiding it. It can be equally difficult to manage what you say to yourself and others. Next, my friend the parrot will share insight into your self-talk, which can impact what people think of themselves.

Additional Resources

- *Crucial Conversations* by Paterson, Grenny, McMillan and Switzler.

- *The 12 Week Year* by Brian Moran and Michael Lennington.

- *Indistractable: How to Control Your Attention and Choose Your Life* by Nir Eyal.

The Parrot

Self-Talk and the Rumor Mill

"People may not remember what you say,
but they will remember how you made them feel."

Maya Angelou

Alexander William Kinglake is credited with the sentiment, *"Stick and stones may break my bones, but words can never hurt me."* Or can they? Do you remember your parents or someone telling you this as a kid? It is true that sticks and stones and a plethora of other things can break your bones. It's important to be wary of something else, too. Your self-talk runs amok on the inside while the rumor mill works its "magic" on the outside. There may or may not be truth in your words or rumors, however, they can have an immense amount of influence on you. Our team has found words can hurt many times more and last so much longer than a broken bone. A broken bone can heal faster than one's broken heart, spirit, or confidence. Regardless of who you're talking to, whether it's a team member, a family member, or yourself, it's important to think about what you say and how you say it. Words can have a positive or negative effect on people. As a parrot, I am superb when it comes to repeating things because that's what I do. I listen and repeat what I heard or think I heard you say to yourself. Sometimes I say the same thing over and over again, maybe for years. Other times my messages can be locked away in silence, showing up at the most inopportune times.

I have several names depending on whom you may be talking to or who's writing about me. Some call me the negative voice, the naysayer, your inner critic, or saboteur. When referring to the positive self-talk voice inside of me, I've been called your champion. I'd rather be your champion and build you up with humble confidence than to tear you down when you allow your inner critic or your saboteur to chime into the conversation.

I'm in charge of self-talk and the rumor mill. I am a master at repeating what I hear others say and in what you choose to say to yourself. I repeat what I hear sometimes without checking out the validity of the information. It's amazing to me that people seem to remember the negative things they hear and especially what they say to themselves about themselves, even when it may not be true. I remember a line from the movie *Pretty Woman* that Julia Roberts said to Richard Gere. She said, "The bad stuff is easier to believe. You ever notice that?"

What do you say to yourself, either consciously or subconsciously? Does your self-talk tend to be on the positive or on the negative side? Why is it we hear the negative and continue to repeat it, while the positive is harder to believe? Some of the common things I hear people repeat to themselves are, "I can't, I don't know how, am I good enough? I'm not as...(you fill in the blank)." The list goes on and on. Are you allowing constant negative talk to hinder your success?

But it's not all bad! I have many positive things to say, too. You just don't let me repeat them as often as the negatives. What might you possibly be saying over and over that isn't true? It's just you've said it so long you believe it. It's tough to change, yet I give people choices about what they repeat to themselves and others. I have a splendid memory and can help you remember things that are both good and bad. The trick is to work on listening to the positive things your self-talk has to say and not let yourself get caught up in the negative. When you constantly tell yourselves you don't have what it takes or allow self-doubt to creep in, you get into trouble and begin to believe it.

When Ann went through her Life and Leadership Coaching certification at Coach for Life, Peter always encouraged everyone to focus more on the 98 percent, the good and positive thoughts, and less on the two percent where the more negative ones tend to hang out and where your snake usually lives. Peter said what you focus on expands, so if you focus on what you want to do or how you want to be and feel, you'll keep doing it or working on it until you begin to believe it. Ann asks her clients not what they are doing "wrong" (because it's not that it's wrong) but what it is they want more of or to do more of. What you focus on does expand.

It's kind of like when Ann was working on this book. You should have heard all the things she heard me saying to her. The thing is I had plenty of good things to say about writing a book; it just took her awhile to listen to them and change her self-talk. One of her friends, Stan, suggested that she write down why she wanted to write this book and how she hoped people felt after reading it and post it where she could see it every day. She reads it often. One of her other favorite words she uses in her self-talk is "yet." If she doesn't know how to do something, she says, "I don't know how to do it, *yet*." Change is hard! And it has a lot of steps. The first step is being aware of what you're saying to yourself and others. The second step, decide to take action. The third step is to take action and begin.

The book *Crucial Conversations* is a great resource for examining the stories you tell yourself. Patterson, Grenny, McMillan, and Switzler challenge readers to keep a pulse on their thoughts. Do you play the victim? Do you stop to think about whether you had or what role you may have played in the situation? Do you blame or exaggerate what the other person did and assume the worst before talking with the person? Do you look at yourself as powerless over a situation and not even looking for healthy and positive alternatives? The authors do a great job in talking about the stories you tell yourself. Even if you have confidence, sometimes life happens and your self-talk, the inner critic, takes over and can flood your mind with negative thoughts and create self-doubt even though you may know it's not true. You can flip the switch and choose the positive.

Based on Ann's experience and talking to many people throughout her career, positive self-talk can support you in feeling confident in yourself, and negative self-talk can mentally paralyze you.

Where does *your* self-talk come from?
- Childhood—what your peers said to you?
- Parents—what your parents said and didn't say?
- Peers?
- Supervisors?
- Friends?
- Your own beliefs about yourself?
- Experiences—personal and professional?

Maybe you haven't mastered or even learned a skill or have the experience you need—yet—meaning it's one of those weaknesses which still needs to be developed to become a strength. It's all in what you say and continue to repeat to yourself. Ann loves the power of yet. She remembers when working on this book she used to say, "I don't know this," or "I haven't done that," blah, blah, blah. When she added one simple, yet important word, it changed her entire mindset. Ironically, she just used the word in the prior sentence: YET!

She now includes "yet" in how she talks to herself, friends, and her team. For example, she doesn't know how to create and produce a podcast, yet. She's going to learn because it's something on her bucket list and plan for the future. The power of yet. Three letters, one word. It can help get you in the right frame of mind. Same goes for how you work and collaborate with your team members. When they indicate they don't know something, add the word yet. It can and will help them realize they can accomplish their goal. It provides hope for those who are facing challenges or a new job or responsibilities in their position or life-changing event.

What you say to your peers, friends, or your children can have a long-lasting effect on their self-esteem, how they view you and themselves, as well as the workplace, even what their parrots say daily to them.

Self-talk and your thoughts can provide insight into who you think you are and who you want to be. It can subconsciously influence what you think, feel, and how you act for better or worse. It can impact who you want to become.

The Rumor Mill

Masters of words, I, your parrot, embrace repeating what I hear. I listen and am observant. However, I don't necessarily listen to understand or respond when I hear what is said and repeat it regardless of the validity. Not only do I show up in your head, I also show up at work and sometimes among friends.

Do you know people who repeat what they hear regardless of whether or not they have taken the time to research the truth? Darn rumor mill. It can make or break an office or even families and friendships. Ann once worked somewhere where the rumor mill ran rampant. Sometimes things were true and sometimes they were things people thought to be true, but they weren't.

Why do you think rumors begin? Someone once told Ann that rumors begin because people don't have enough or accurate information. It's not that people are trying to sabotage anything, they just want to belong and be in the "know," so they share information because information can be powerful and influential. Unlike me, the rumor mill can alter the information because people are human, and they forget what was really said or add in what they believe to be true.

What can you do to ensure the "rumors" contain the truth and accurate information? Keep yourself and your team members up to date with accurate information.

If you don't know or aren't at liberty to share at the moment—tell people you don't know, and you'll share as soon as you are able. Make yourself a note so you remember to follow through with your promises.

As a leader and positive team member, it's up to you to determine what you are going to say to yourself and your other team members. It's also important to decide what you will do when you hear something that either you know is not true or aren't certain whether or not it is. If what your gut or intuition are saying doesn't sound quite right, it probably isn't. It's up to you whether or not you are going to take part in spreading the rumor, investigate the information, and then share what is true. It's not always going to be easy, and no one said being a leader or doing the right thing was, but it's worth it.

You can control what your parrot says to you over and over again, as well as, if you will be a positive influence in the rumor mill.

One Word: Two Perspectives

An acquaintance of Ann's shared with her a comment someone made to him a long time ago when he was young, which was hurtful and uncomfortable. It stuck with him for years. When people told him that he was funny, he took offense. When asked what it was about that statement that bothered him, he shared this. He felt as if he was being compared to a joker—not to be taken seriously. This weighed on him for years.

Ann asked him if it was possible people meant he had a good sense of humor and made them smile and feel better about life in the moment. He pondered it and decided to think about it. Ann encouraged him to contact four to five people in the manner he felt comfortable (via email or verbally) and ask them to share five characteristics about him they admired and appreciated. Three of the five people shared he was funny and had a great sense of humor. He made them smile or laugh and had a great way of lightening the moment.

It took a great deal of courage for him to do this. However, decades of hearing a phrase in his self-talk, as well as from others, changed because of a new perspective. He shared with Ann that because of the activity he had a new appreciation for being "funny." His self-talk didn't tell him he was a joker or not taken seriously. It began telling him he brought smiles and joy to others.

A Dad that Shared an Unfortunate and Damaging Thought

Ann learned about a dad who had told his kids those who come from broken homes do not amount to anything. Several years later, the parents of those kids went through a divorce. Yep, you guessed it, one of their kiddos, a pre-teen at the time, asked if they were going to lose everything because of what was said to him in the early years. Why anyone would ever say that is a mystery. However, I repeat what I hear. Don't get me wrong, we all make mistakes and say things we don't mean. I think this is a good example of how words can influence people in all stages and areas of life.

I remember people making fun of Ann for ideas she had or thoughts she shared. This happens at home and at the workplace. It only needs to happen once, and people can shut down for an undisclosed amount of time, maybe even forever. So what if an idea isn't the greatest? Maybe it will be the one that inspires the idea that is chosen. People may refrain from sharing if they feel they have been ridiculed or criticized, and they may convince themselves, "I have nothing to share." In reality, they do have something to share and during the next brainstorming session or discussion that same person, with the "interesting" idea, may have the ultimate solution. Build people up, don't tear them down or fill their heads with things that aren't true.

Mom's Advice and Support System

Ann's mom used to tell her she had two ears and one mouth for a reason. Close one and open two and she would be surprised at what she might learn. The challenge in some cases is deciphering what is true and what is not. What to believe and what not to believe.

I remember when Ann finally got serious and wrote her first book (this one) and decided she would host a podcast in the future. Her self-talk ran rampant in her head. Who was she to write a book? What did she have to say or share with people? What if they didn't like it? Yet what if they did? She wouldn't know unless she tried. There were plenty of challenges in acknowledging her own self-talk as it took on a life of its own.

Ann is fortunate to have a great support system. For years, she was a member of the Jaycees, where she learned leadership skills, gained wonderful experiences, and made great lifelong friends. She is part of an amazing group of coaches with ICF Iowa and attends training and masterminds led by Mitch Matthews, who is one of the most positive and encouraging people she knows. They authentically share, with not only her, but all members, that each has their own unique gift and message to offer the world. Go out and share it. Those who need to hear it will. Those who don't won't. One message Ann works to include in her memory and share is, "Remember you have something to offer people, as do your peers." Words and stories can weigh you down or lift you up. It's up to you to decide what you will do. It's important to remember most people don't purposely say things to hurt people. If you have, don't beat yourself up. Acknowledge it, address it, apologize, if need be, learn from it, and move on—working to be aware of self-talk, what you say to others, and future rumor mills.

Lessons Learned

- Self-talk is important.

- It's important to pay attention to what we say to ourselves and to and about others.

- You have the power to choose what you say and help others learn to make choices.

- Remember to ask and sometimes reframe what and how you say things to others and yourself. Is it kind? Is it true? Is it positive? Is it helpful or hurtful?

- Words and stories can weigh us down or lift us up. It's up to you and me to decide what they will do. It's important to remember most people don't purposely say things to hurt people.

- The rumor mill exists on the inside and outside. Acknowledge it and that it can have a positive or negative effect on you and your team. Then do something about it.

- Decide what you are going to allow self-talk to repeat over and over? What "rumors" will you spread and which ones will you squelch? What will you allow to be repeated to others?

My Strengths

- I inspire you to ask yourself tough questions.

- I help you ask yourself what's important to remember and what do you need to ignore?

- I encourage you to decide who and what you will and won't listen to as well as share with others.

Your Strengths (List the strengths you see in yourself when it comes to recognizing and managing your self-talk as well as what's being said by the rumor mill.)

Strategies: Choose the one(s) which will best serve you.

- Listen to the words and tone of voice you use when sharing information and feedback with yourself and others.

- Be cognizant of what you tell yourself over and over again.

- Contact four or five of the people who you trust and who you know will be honest as well as positive. Ask them to share four or five things they believe you do well or make look effortless. This may be most comfortable to do via email. Tell them you've been asked to conduct a simple activity. This will help you remember what you do well. Refer to this list often, especially if your self-talk needs some assistance. This helps with confidence, too.

- Name your positive self-talk.

- Name your negative self-talk. When he/she shows up—Tell him/her to be quiet.

- Evaluate whether what you're telling yourself is really true or if you are allowing self-doubt to creep in.

- Be aware of the stories you tell yourself.

- Ask yourself questions such as:
  - Is this true?
  - Do I really believe what my head is telling me?
  - Is this what I want to be saying to myself?
  - What can and am I willing to do to monitor, control and change the stories in my head?
  - What do others say that I then repeat to myself?
  - What do I want my self-talk to sound like?

- Think before you share information.
- Talk to someone you trust about the stories you hold deep within.
  - Determine the most appropriate person to talk to based on the situation. It might be a counselor, a leadership coach, family member, friend, or a supervisor.
- Acknowledge the rumor mill exists. Then manage and even use it, if appropriate. For example, Ann worked for a major non-profit that underwent a major reorganization. One strategy used throughout the process—they established a communication committee. The transitional management team, after making decisions, provided updates to the communication committee. One of the committee's major responsibilities was to share information with their peers. The Transitional Management Team then emailed everyone with information regarding decisions made. Many had questions about the new structure. For some reason, staff members asked their peers and not their supervisors or those on the Transitional Management Team their questions. How were those who would serve on the communications committee chosen? They were chosen based on positions held and the respect they had among their peers. Staff periodically went to them for advice and information. Better to have accurate information circulating than stories made up because the information was not available or shared.

- Journal and do some self-reflection. It helps to see things in writing. Here are some questions you can ask yourself:
  - How do I talk to and what do I continue to say myself?
  - How do I talk to my friends? Spouse? Partner? Children?
  - How do I talk to my peers? Supervisor? Direct reports?
  - What if anything do I repeat? Is it true? Is it going to hurt someone?
  - How does what I say affect me, and the team with whom I work?
  - How does what I share benefit others?
  - Write the story you are telling yourself. Read it. Wad it up. Throw it away.
  - Write the story you want to tell yourself. Read it again and again and again until it is the story that's automatically in your head.

Your Reflection

Reflection Questions: Answer here or in a separate journal.

1. What am I going to do to create and listen to more positive self-talk and reduce the negative stories I tell myself?

2. How will I help to contain the rumor mill at work?

3. How does my parrot show up? Does he talk to me in a positive tone and with words of affirmation? Or does he repeat the bad or negative stuff?

Your Biggest Take-away(s) Regarding Self-Talk and the Rumor Mill

Your Action Plan

Here is an example of what your action plan may look like. Remember it's your plan not mine, this is only an example to support you in getting started. Choose the action that will support you in moving forward. There is space for you to write your personal plan of action at the end of the example.

1. *Goal: To recognize when my self-talk is not serving me.*

2. *Action: As soon as I hear myself doubting my ability I will stop and examine the reason for my doubts or negative self-talk. I will re-frame what I am saying to myself. I will also surround myself with positive quotes I can easily see.*

3. *Who will support me? I have to recognize the thoughts and then be willing to talk to someone about them. For example: my book coach helps me work through challenging thoughts and asks me questions about the reason I am having them. I then refer to my list of strengths and determine what I do want to tell myself. My best friend can support me in remembering what I do have to offer.*

4. *Date: I will begin today.*

5. *How will I know I'm making progress? My self-talk will be more positive, and I won't beat myself up as much. I will feel more confident.*

Your Turn: Answer here or in a separate journal.

1. Goal:

2. Action:

3. Who can support you?

4. Date to begin:

5. How will you know you made progress?

Whew. I don't know about you, but it can be exhausting thinking about all the things we've been talking about. The next team member is all about laughter and relaxation which are more important in life that we may give them credit for. So, let's meet my friend, the playful puppy.

Additional Resources

- *Crucial Conversations* by Kerry Patterson, Joseph Grenny, Ron McMillan, Al Switzler.

- *Positive Intelligence* by Shirzad Chamine.

- *Stop Overthinking, Master Your Emotions & Start Taking Action: The Ultimate Guide to Stop Unproductive Thoughts, Beat Negativity and Unlock Your Unlimited Potential by Taking Decisive Action* by Brilliant Thinking.

The Puppy

Laughter, Loyalty, and Relaxation

"A day without laughter is a day wasted."

Charlie Chaplin

When I met the geese, it was easy for me to share what I, as the puppy, brought to the team. Laughter, Loyalty, and Relaxation. Who wouldn't want more of these three traits in their lives? I think everyone wants more of what I have to offer, yet they're not as easy to bring to the team as you might think, especially as you get older and have more responsibilities added to your plate. I'm lucky. I get to share and provide more of the fun characteristics with you.

Laughter

Do you like to laugh and have fun? I do. I laugh at myself all the time! Do you know people who have a great sense of humor, love to laugh, and bring laughter to the world? Me, too. Who brings laughter to your life? To whose life do you bring joy and laughter? Granted, we are not responsible for other people's happiness just as others are not responsible for *our* happiness. Each person is responsible for their own happiness. However, family and friends can surely add happiness to your life just like you add to theirs.

You might be wondering how laughter fits into leading the team within. Having fun and relaxing is important! It energizes us. I've heard that kids laugh over four hundred

143

times a day, whereas adults laugh only around fifteen times a day. How sad is that? After Ann had her son, her laughter increased daily because not only was he funny, but he laughed all the time. All work and no play make for a long day and life. If it was up to me, we would laugh and play all day. But then my other team members may not get to use their superpowers to support you in living your best life. So, I'm thinking about working hard, and making time to play hard is a win. Reach a happy medium. You don't have to party all night but take time to play. Bring joy and fun into the workplace!

What if you find someone who only wants to have fun and not work or puts their work last? How do you lead yourself and others? I think it's important to ask people questions about what's important to them. Ann talked with someone and after several questions, they finally uncovered what would motivate him to study first and play later. Money. If he studied, he would pass his classes. If he didn't, he would have to repeat the class, which meant paying for it a second time. The solution? He agreed for each class passed, he would set aside $200 toward a new phone instead of spending $1,800 on taking a class for a second time.

I wonder why people don't take time to do something they enjoy every day. I remember hearing Ann say to her son that she would like to "play" more or work on pictures when he was little. His response was as simple and honest as they come, "Well then, just do it." There's something to be said for just doing it. Though I know it's challenging when in your mind there's so much you feel that has to be done and is still to do!

Loyalty

One of my other traits is loyalty. I am said to be man's best friend. It's important to think about the people to whom or things to which you want to be loyal. It's a value important to most, and it is one of the leadership traits to manage. What does it mean to be loyal? Years ago, it seemed as if people stayed with a company for the majority of their career. Today, not so much. There are pros and cons to both. No matter where you are or for whom you work or with whom you live, you get to choose to whom or what you want to be loyal. Maintaining confidentiality is part of loyalty. Occasionally, you may have to choose where you place your loyalty. Through time and experience, Ann learned that knowing what your core values are and remaining loyal to yourself is the first step and is not to be taken lightly.

Loyalty fuels belonging and trust. It supports you in making personal and professional decisions. It's not always as easy as it sounds. To whom and where do you want your loyalty to lie?

Relaxation

What do we do when we have too much fun or want to only relax and not do the work we know needs or has to be done? Like editing drafts of a book, writing a paper, or preparing for a presentation? It's fun to think about writing a paper or a presentation. It's fun to write the first draft. It's fun and exciting to see it in print. It's not as much fun editing it and going through the details.

Is it easy for you to relax or do you have to work at it? Are you challenged with relaxing? Ann is. I am not.

She's embarrassed to say she has to work to relax. Her dad was a workaholic. He grew up during the depression and didn't have much as a kid. He worked for everything he had. That's why material things were important to him as an adult. Ann is a recovering workaholic, not because she didn't have things when she grew up, but I think because she worked closely with her dad in his business. At times, this mindset serves her well. At others, not so much.

Throughout the pandemic, people were challenged with different things. In working to offer workshops and classes online and with clients using a variety of platforms, it was very stressful working to learn Zoom, WebEx, Teams, and so on. In listening to the puppy, Ann finally took a few hours off and made herself a promise to take time off so she would not only be more productive but a lot more fun to live with, if you know what I mean.

Can you think of a team member you work with or used to work with that likes to have fun? Sometimes it was too much fun in that it seemed hard to get your work done. Granted, some people will relax first and then work and if that works, does it matter—unless, of course, it's during the workday. Then it's important to work hard and get the job done first.

Do you have to work at achieving a balance or, as some say, alignment between work and play? Are you a workaholic? There's no judgment. We are who we are. We can change if we want to. That does not mean it will be easy. Working hard, having fun, relaxing, and laughing are important. With so many people working at home and continuing to work at home now that the pandemic is mostly behind us, it will be even more crucial that we learn to balance work and play and help them live in harmony with each other.

College Roommates Have Way too Much Fun Before Finals

In college, one night before finals, Ann and her girlfriends went to a party. About midnight, a couple of friends left to get a good night's sleep. Ann and one of her friends allowed me to talk them into staying out all night long, though I had help with this because there were several others from the party that weren't ready to call it a night. They ended up staying and hanging out all night with friends, returning home in time to shower and make it to class to take their exams. Not her most intelligent decision. It may have been a good idea to listen to the *wise old owl team member* but hey, when you're young, invincible, and haven't learned to listen to everyone on the team yet, the one who yells the loudest or is the squeaky wheel gets oiled and has the most influence. By the way, she managed to pass all her exams that day though she never pulled an all-night party the night before exams again.

Bob and Daisy — Loyalty

During the writing of this book, Julie, a friend of Ann's, posted a picture on Facebook of Bob, her dad, and Daisy, his dog, lying at his feet while he peacefully slept. Julie had taken Daisy to the assisted-living home so he could see her dad one last time. Except for a couple of trips to visit the lawn, Daisy refused to leave his side, instinctively knowing when she left, she would never see him again. The staff allowed Daisy to spend the night. Bob passed away the next day at age 95. He lived a great life. Daisy was his companion for years. I don't share this to bring sadness. I share this because the loyalty of a friend who stands with us during the best of times and worst of times is to be treasured. The never-ending smiles and contentment they bring are priceless.

Loyalty is the quality of staying firm in your values, friendship, and support for someone or something.

Ann, Doug, and the Deer — One Word + Two Perceptions = Conflict or Comedy?

Driving to a Jaycee meeting in Sioux City, Ann and Doug had just left McDonalds and headed up I-29. Ann was in the driver's seat, Doug, a passenger, suddenly shouted, "Watch the deer!"

Startled, Ann looked at the deer and watched it dart between cars across their side of the interstate and into the southbound lanes safely reaching the other side. Exasperated, Doug asked, "What are you doing?"

Ann replied, perplexed, "What do you mean what I am I doing? You said watch the deer, so I did. We didn't hit it. We're safe. The deer is safe. What's the problem?"

With a heavy sigh and shaking his head, Doug said matter-of-factly, "Not that deer. The one that's probably following it. Deer is plural. They run in pairs."

Ann calmly stated, "You said watch the deer, and that is precisely what I did."

Same language. Same word. Two people who understood the word and listened to each other. Two entirely different messages were heard that night. Perhaps this is the reason Doug prefers to drive now wherever they travel.

To this day they don't let perception get in their way when communicating. Not to say there aren't still misunderstandings, because there are. However, each can still laugh with the other when they hear the same thing and understand something totally different.

Lessons Learned

- Laughter, loyalty, and relaxation are important. They can strengthen your team and enhance life in general. When we are having fun and relaxing, we are re-energizing. As Stephen Covey might say, we are making deposits in our emotional bank account.
- Work hard.
- Play hard.
- Celebrate life.
- Do something that brings you joy each day. It doesn't have to take a long time, but take *some* time.
- Don't just check things off the list.
- Stop and smell the roses.
- Enjoy the journey.

God promised a safe landing, not necessarily an easy passage. With loyalty and laughter from and with friends, the joys are more joyful and sorrows less stressful.

My Strengths

- Loyally to myself and others.
- Laughter and fun.
- Relaxation.

Your Strengths (List the strengths you see in yourself when it comes to laughter, loyalty, and relaxation.)

Strategies: Choose the one(s) which will best serve you.

- Work hard—play hard.
- Take a break or do something with a friend or for yourself.
- Work first, then relax (think how good it will feel to make progress then play—less chance of the monkey hanging out on your back).
- Have potlucks at work.
- Celebrate birthdays and anniversaries at home and work.
- Enjoy a virtual coffee break, lunch, or happy hour with friends and coworkers.
- Enjoy a bingo ice breaker at an event.
- Begin each meeting with everyone sharing something they are celebrating or looking forward to in the next few months.
- Maintain confidentiality.
- Take a quick walk.
- Call a friend.
- Read a book.
- Meditate.
- Do a crossword puzzle.
- Work on a jigsaw puzzle.
- Write in a gratitude journal.
- Pay someone a compliment.
- Pay yourself a compliment.

- Find people with similar interests—start a card club. Ann and her husband are one of six couples who play cards once a month. During the pandemic thanks to Jay, we found the Euchre app and played on our phones and zoomed with each other. Next best thing to being there in person. They are blessed as they all laugh most of the night. There are a couple of couples who are regular subs, and they are just as much a part of the card club as the six original couples. Each individual is loyal to all others.

- Create a dinner club—go out every so often with friends and try new and different restaurants. If it gets too expensive, take turns having potlucks and game nights. Board games are a personal favorite of Ann's.

- Girls (or Boys) Night Out—get together and talk, eat, play games, see a movie—okay, the boys may play a card game or two and the girls may play Bunco. Let's face it—it's not about the game, it's about the camaraderie, the food, the fun, and most importantly the friendships.

- Create time for fun.

- Have a game night (Rumikub and Things are two favorite board games)

- Do something that brings you joy each day.

- Organize a lunch bunch—enjoy lunch out or brown-bag it once a week.

- Share jokes within reason and when appropriate. Know your audience and surroundings (Joe).

Your Reflection

Reflection Questions: Answer here or in a separate journal.

1. What brings me joy and laughter?
2. To whom or what am I most loyal?
3. Who are those most loyal to me?
4. Do I work to relax, or does it come easy for me?
5. What do I do to relax?

Your Biggest Take-Away(s) Regarding Laughter, Loyalty, and Relaxation

Your Action Plan

Here is an example of what your action plan may look like. Remember it's your plan not mine, this is only an example to support you in getting started. Choose the action which will support you in moving forward. There is space for you to write your personal plan of action at the end of the example.

1. *Goal: Take time to relax and do at least one thing that brings me joy each day.*
2. *Action: Set aside time daily to do something I enjoy. I enjoy watching Wheel of Fortune, reading, and jigsaw puzzles. I will spend 30 minutes a day doing at least one of the things mentioned in the prior sentence.*
3. *Who will support me? My husband.*
4. *Date: Begin today.*
5. *How will I know I'm making progress? I will see my bookmark move forward in my book, my puzzle will be taking shape, or I will recognize that I have watched an episode of Wheel of Fortune.*

Your Turn: Answer here or in a separate journal.

1. Goal:

2. Action:

3. Who can support you?

4. Date to begin:

5. How will you know you made progress?

I sure hope you had fun thinking about and planning what you're going to do to have more fun in life. Dreaming about and choosing what you want to work on next can be fun too. Next, let's see how my friend, the rabbit who gives us choices, can help us move forward and choose what we want to focus on next.

Additional Resources

- *The Energy Bus* by Jon Gordon.
- *First Things First* by Stephen Covey.
- *Humor That Works* by Andrew Tarvin.
- *Play: How It Shapes the Brain, Opens the Imagination, and Invigorates the Soul* by Dr. Stuart Brown.
- *Finding Joy* by Carrie Copley.
- *Hugh Jackman and the Joy Revolution* by Louisa Joy Dykstra.

The Rabbit

Choosing Priorities and Setting Goals

"If you chase two rabbits, both will get away."

Unknown

Big Goals. Bold Goals. Two Major Goals. Where to begin? Granted, you probably have multiple goals and countless projects on which you're working and that most likely won't change. Whether it is in your personal or professional life, most people have a couple of big dreams and goals on which they want to work and achieve. Big goals take planning, time, and energy. We all have 24 hours in a day. Most work, in or outside the home, and have many responsibilities. So, what happens when you have two major goals; each of which is important? Do you chase both at the same time or one at a time?

Do you feel as if there aren't enough hours in a day? Does your head spin with ideas and all the things you want to do and dreams you want and will achieve? Ever want to say, "My brain and plate are full?" Perhaps they are overflowing. You're thinking you have so much to do, you're not sure where to start or on what to focus. Or better yet, you work on so many things at once you don't feel as if you're gaining ground or accomplishing any of them. I get it.

Like my other friends in this book, I have a quote about me that makes me famous. I bet you've heard it and can relate: "if you chase two rabbits, both will get away." Sound familiar? Yep, I'm the rabbit, who people have been chasing for years and who works closely with the other rabbits who provide you with ideas and choices.

When I met the geese, they helped me realize the value and importance of giving you choices, and yet how working on one goal at a time and focusing serves you well. Sometimes your "goals" show up as two areas of priorities in life and you may have to choose to put one on the back burner. I'll share more later in the chapter when Kevin, a friend of Ann's, shares his story of choosing where to invest his time and finding peace with his decision.

When I show up, there's usually more than one of me. It's our job to bring the big goals to your attention. The challenge is my friends and I entice you to chase two or more big goals at once. Most people work on multiple projects during any given time. It's the size of the goal, time needed to achieve the goal(s), and capacity you have at any given moment which can influence what you decide to work on and impact your success. There's nothing wrong with having more than one goal you're working on at once. It's just hard when you try to pursue two major goals or projects at the same time. People have many reasons for chasing more than one goal at the same time. For one it's exciting to have multiple interests and goals.

What are some of the major goals people may be pursuing? Some may want to write a book, others get a new job, start their own business or non-profit, or remodel the house. It may be a major decision of whether to return to school, stay in school, leave a career, and work part-time or stay home full-time with your little one until they go to school. What if you have two businesses you want to pursue? Ever try to excel at both? It can be overwhelming, challenging, and extremely frustrating working on too many major projects or goals at the same time.

I show up in Ann's team more often than not. Teaching, earning a coaching certification, taking classes and courses, growing her business, starting a podcast, the list of goals went on and on, of goals Ann wanted to accomplish. Then of course add to the list that Ann had always wanted to write a book. There's a lot more information about this shared from my friend the Monkey's point of view in the chapter focused on procrastination. However, chasing too many 'rabbits' at one time is not only a challenge for Ann and many people, but it can also hinder you from accomplishing what you want in a timely manner.

I'm not here to tell you what to do. I'm here to share that I give you choices. It's up to you which one you want to focus on. The geese taught Ann how listening to what I have to say, making a choice, focusing on one big goal, achieving it, and then moving on to the next can be freeing, exhilarating, and bring you peace of mind.

By the way, between you and me, I think she finally got tired of just thinking about writing a book. Her husband was probably tired of hearing about it. She finally figured it was Time for her to get off the pot and decide to act or let the idea of writing a book go and move on.

Why do you and others chase more than one goal at a time? There could be a variety of reasons. Here are several possibilities:

- You're interested in achieving both goals.

- The goals are exciting to think about achieving.

- You want it all and more appears to be better. But is more really better? In this day and age sometimes it feels like it, but is it? Isn't it more satisfying to do one thing well rather than try to do too many things at once and not feel successful at any of them?

- You like to do a variety of things and have multiple interests. So does Ann, but the sad truth is there are only so many—24 to be exact—hours in a day and only so much energy to go around. For example, can you write two books at once? Maybe, but can you do them well and will you finish either? Ann thought she could write two books at once. I guess technically she could and believe me, she tried. Yet neither book was getting finished. Frustration grew. Asking for help is difficult for most. However, once Ann read the book *Published* by Chandler Bolt, joined Self-Publishing School, and got a Book/Author Coach she realized if she was going to write the second book with Noah, her son, she needed to finish the first one. She even asked herself if she was more excited about the idea of authoring a book than actually writing it. Tough question to ask but a necessary one.

The geese know where they're going and are all working together to get to the same goal or destination. My friends, the other rabbits, want your attention. At times, it can be exhilarating having all these projects and things on which to work. Other times, it can be exhausting not feeling as if you're not reaching any of your goals or finishing anything. Maybe you've just gone through the motions to get it checked off your list and not done your best or enjoyed the process.

So many priorities. So little time. It is true if you chase two of us, both will get away. By the way, that doesn't mean you can't have us both. You just may not be able to have us at the same time.

Challenges Faced in Achieving the Big Goals

Determining on which goal to focus on first and which one to let get away—for now.

Priorities and determining which one needs our attention today can be difficult. As we also know, priorities change. Sometimes hourly. Sometimes daily. Sometimes weekly. Sometimes based on our supervisor's or organization's focus. Sometimes it depends upon the season of life in which you find yourself. It's good to acknowledge you have multiple projects and things you want to do. Embrace it. Manage it. Lead me and don't let me lead you down a rabbit hole. Keep your sanity, or at least some of it.

Being overwhelmed. Sometimes when Ann is overwhelmed, she does nothing or does mindless things to make her think she's accomplishing something.

The details. They challenge Ann. She, like many people, loves to create new ideas and is excited at the beginning when the goal is new and exhilarating and again at the end when the project is complete. She loves the sense of accomplishment. Who doesn't? It's not the hard work that's an issue, it's the messy middle with all the details, which aren't as exciting as the ideas. Is your head spinning with all your dreams and ideas? Do you ever feel pulled in a million different directions? That, of course, may be my friend the squirrel. You begin working on one project only to be distracted by another, which may, in fact, need your attention. The list goes on and on. However, if your focus keeps changing, you might never finish anything. It's kind of like this book. However, if you're reading it, Ann found a way to finish it. She found herself jumping from one idea to the next, and alas—it was years down the road, and she still had plenty of ideas; however, she didn't have a book written on any of them. Sound familiar? I get it. So, what's keeping people from focusing? Maybe all the ideas are good ones, but there's only so much time in a day and bandwidth in our brains.

Deciding which road to take. I took Alice down the rabbit hole in Lewis Carroll's books, *Alice in Wonderland* and *Through the Looking-Glass.* One day, Alice was running around Wonderland, chasing me. She came to a fork in the road. She stopped. She thought. She contemplated which road to take. She asked herself, loud enough for those close to her to hear, "Which path do I take?"

Sitting in the tree watching and listening was the extremely wise Cheshire Cat. Slowly he stretched his legs, and with a wide grin on his face and deep sigh he asked, "Well Alice, where are you going?"

Alice replied, "I don't really know."

He smiled and simply stated, "Then it doesn't really matter which road you take."

This is so true. If you don't know where you're going, it doesn't matter which of us you chase. The path which will lead you to success is determined by what is important and on what success looks like to you. Some questions that may help you make your decision are:

- What is it you want to achieve?

- What season of life are you in and how long will you stay there?

- What other priorities and time commitments do you have right now that are non-negotiable and important?

- Which goal(s) are the most important?

- What will you regret not doing?

I like to have your attention and want you to chase all your dreams at the same time, because I want you to be happy and successful. Sometimes you have to choose what to work on and when. It's about priorities and choices. Not easy, but doable.

The good news about me is I provide you with ideas, opportunities, and choices, so when you finish one goal or project, you reevaluate and choose which project or activity you want to pursue next. This does not mean we forget about things for which we are responsible. It means we need to be aware of how many things we go after at once. I like to see people busy. Busy is not synonymous with being productive. There is a difference. For most, it's about being productive. Each of you defines what it means to be productive for yourself. I've seen people busy, but not moving forward on their goals. Have you ever felt like this?

Saying no to a goal today doesn't mean you are saying no forever. When you say no to one thing, it means you get to say yes to something else. And that something else can bring you immense joy, satisfaction, and a sense of accomplishment. It can be a relief to focus on one major goal.

Like the four seasons, the seasons of our lives bring different priorities and opportunities. My take on the seasons is that spring is a time of hope, new life, and growth. Many farm babies are born. Summer is a time to relax and recharge. Ironically, depending on the season of life or where you live, it can be super busy working to cram all the outdoor activities in before the snow falls. Fall is a time for transformation. We are reminded by the changing leaves that we can change if we want or if we believe a change is needed. Winter. Hmmm, winter is the least favorite season for many. Depending on where you live, it can be cold and dark. However, it can be a time to slow down, reflect, and enjoy being at home.

God blessed Ann with a wealth of ideas and dreams. I'm confident you are also blessed with a wide variety of things you want to pursue. I want you to go after your goals and achieve them. That's one reason I have so many friends. We are the ideas you want to pursue. The challenge is deciding what to pursue when.

Have you had to make a choice on what to pursue? Maybe you're facing a tough choice between two paths today. You have it within you to make the best choice possible with what you know today. When you say no, you may have less chaos in your mind, therefore giving you the ability to concentrate on your priorities at any given time or season in your life.

One activity Ann developed and uses is a process called— Ideas, Action, and Satisfaction. The first step is where you list your ideas and decide which one you want to pursue first. Second, make a list of actions you need to take to turn that idea into a reality and include a timeline. Third, write your idea or goal as if you've already achieved it. Fourth, list the potential obstacles and what you can do to overcome them. Fifth, list how and with whom you're going to celebrate. If you want the handout, it's available for free on her website. www.annwrightsolutions.com/freegift

"If it was easy, everyone would be doing it."

Unknown

You got this.

Ann, School, and the Jaycees

Each of us has our own journey, priorities, and decisions to make on where we want to focus our time and energy. People have their own path to follow or create. In her early and mid-twenties, Ann's career was her focus. If she wanted to be a District Manager, she knew she had to change stores and cities to get to the position she wanted. Once she achieved her goal and then married, she did not want to move every couple of years.

Soon after her first marriage ended in divorce, she found herself working full-time, going to school part-time, and active in the Jaycees. Volunteering and sharpening her skills as a leader were important to her. As an active member of the Iowa Jaycees, she was blessed with many opportunities.

At the time, I served her well. There were many opportunities to gain experience, grow, and figure out what she liked as well as what she didn't. However, when was I a challenge to her? Once it was when she really wanted to run for a state volunteer position in the Jaycees, and then if all worked out, a national volunteer position or go back to school and earn a degree. She still needed to continue working a full-time job, so a choice had to be made. It was not a fun one because I tried to get her to chase earning the degree and volunteering at the same time. Peace of mind and wanting to be successful at what she invested her time caused her to stop, think, and ask herself if she could really have it all at the same time and both the way she wanted. Unfortunately, the answer was no. A choice had to be made.

The question presented itself: did she continue as a volunteer and run for President and maybe National Vice President of a volunteer organization she loved? On the other hand, would it make more sense to return to school full-time (at night) and earn a master's degree as a non-traditional student, which could ultimately help her work part-time and stay home if she was lucky enough to have a family?

There's only so much time in a day and she needed to continue working full-time to support herself. Sitting at a small table in the mall with a Pepsi, Snickers bar, paper, and pen, she made a list of the pros and cons for each decision, then examined them. Looking ahead, contemplating what she wanted her life to look like, she imagined the next three to five years and beyond. Hopefully married again and having children with the chance to stay home and work part time while raising her family was in her future. The choices—return to school or run for State President. Once on paper, the choice was obvious. Go back to school. Short-term pain. Long-term gain.

Changing Careers

Later in life, marrying the second time, having a family became a priority. Once Noah was born and Ann became a mom, she chased a different rabbit. As much as she loved working at the American Cancer Society, she did not want to travel and be gone most of the workweek. She had climbed the ladder society labeled as success. She could be a vice president of a non-profit and a mom at the same time. However, she determined she could not be the vice president and the mom she wanted to be at the same time. What she wanted was to be there during the day with Noah. She did not want to miss those years, no matter what. She could always begin a new career; however, she would never get those first five years back.

So how do you choose between two areas in life that are important? She could have kept doing what she was doing, chasing both rabbits and ignoring the "elephant" in the room, but it was only getting bigger. And to make things more challenging, leaving her job meant drastically changing the budget. Not that money was the deciding factor but let's face it, we all need to live and be realistic.

When contemplating leaving her career and position at the American Cancer Society, as much as she tried to frame things in the positive, for this decision and reflection, she looked at what she would regret more. She looked ahead to when Noah was eighteen and asked herself an important question, "When I look back 20 years from now, will I regret not being a Vice President? Or will I regret not spending time and staying at home when Noah was little and miss most of his waking hours throughout the baby and toddler years? I may regret each of them based on which I choose but what will I regret the most?"

Tough questions. Two options. Tough decision.

In this case, when she looked at the potential regrets, her decision was clear even if the how was not.

After heart-to-heart discussions with her husband and herself, she took a step back and focused on being a mom. Because she returned to school several years before, she had the opportunity to teach part-time at night as an adjunct instructor at a couple of colleges.

Once Noah started school, she switched to teaching one night a week and during the day and facilitating workshops part-time. Being home, being there for Noah, and attending his activities were priorities.

Answering questions provided her with a clear answer, one she remembers to this day when making a tough decision about which of me to chase. "I may have missed continuing as a vice president, but I have *never* regretted leaving my position and spending time with Noah when he was little. For me, there was nothing more important. I look back with a heart of gratitude. There is a picture hanging on my wall made by my sister Susan, given to me by my mom. It states, 'Cleaning and scrubbing can wait 'til tomorrow. For babies grow up we've learned to our sorrow. So quiet down cobwebs. Dust go to sleep. I'm rocking my baby and babies don't keep!'"

As she looks back on the time spent with Noah, it was the right "rabbit" to chase at that time.

To this day, she has no regrets about the decision made.

Seek not to settle for one answer, but question what is important so as not to compromise your values.

"You can have it all, just not at the same time."

Unknown

Kevin's Story: Two Major Goals

Sometimes it's hard to choose which goal to concentrate on first because they are all important. Other choices may seem like "no-brainers." Yet the decision still comes with many emotions and internal challenges. Each goal or choice is important in their own way. Yet there are still only 24 hours in a day and only so much capacity and energy to be had.

Kevin, one of Ann's friends she met at a Next Level Speaker event, shared his story of deciding which "rabbit" to chase first.

Life threw Kevin some curveballs shortly after he left the workshop. In December 2021, his father was diagnosed with a rare brain infection which presented itself as a stroke. He was given three to six months to live.

Kevin's choice: Move to the West Coast to pursue acting and grow his business or stay in Connecticut where he would become his father's daytime caregiver, giving up part of the life he wanted and knew, and yet enjoy and cherish valuable time with his dad. It may seem like the choice was obvious; however, even the most obvious bring challenges. He still needed to earn an income and plan for his own future.

Kevin became a full-time caregiver.

The neurologist from Yale has had seven other patients other than Kevin's dad with the same rare brain infection—only one of them had survived. The doctor tried a one last ditch Hail Mary treatment on Kevin's dad. It worked. His dad is going to be a medical case study at some point. He is already a medical miracle. He still needs help with most things and yet on that brisk fall day that Ann and Kevin talked, Kevin had taken his dad out for a walk for a half hour. After Thanksgiving, his dad suffered a minor heart attack. They are working on what getting back to normal looks like. The good news—as of February 2023, Kevin's Dad was still with us. Kevin and both parents traveled to Disneyworld in March 2023 to celebrate his parents' 50th wedding anniversary.

Kevin has devoted his time to caregiving. He pulled back from clients and reduced time spent on business. One idea Kevin had was to start on a book and as he and Ann know, writing a book is a labor of love and a lot of work. People asked if they were sure they wanted to write a book. For both, it was a big yes and they are supporting each other in moving forward.

In choosing which goal(s) to pursue, I could liken it to the juice fast Kevin does every so often. He shared that it's flushing out the toxins in your body. By sitting down and considering what is important and what to pursue, it's like flushing out the things you don't want or need at the moment, in order to pursue the ones that are the most important to you.

As an entrepreneur you are constantly chasing rabbits. It's deciding which one to chase first that can be a challenge. One of his friends described and referred to my friend, the squirrel. We're all squirrels, running around trying to collect nuts. There are big nuts and little nuts to run after. Kevin, like Ann, has multiple interests, and deciding which to pursue can become incredibly challenging. One thing he discovered recently is to allow his brain to go where its interest lies and remember.

Kevin was a competitive swimmer. He knew what sacrifice felt like and knew he wasn't going to be a professional athlete or an Olympian. Once his college swimming career ended, he pursued his other passion, acting. In the big 50,000-foot view of life, there will be a time and a place for everything. Every dream, every goal has its season—swimmer, actor, a business owner, coach, and now a caregiver, hence Kevin's approach to his dreams, his life, his seasons. There was and will continue to be time to pursue his dreams and goals. Today, at the time of the interview, offered the opportunity to fulfill perhaps the most compelling and important "task"— take care of the man who once took care of him.

Kevin shared that society can skew our view of success. It rates many things as linear, A,B,C,D,E—you get the picture. Yet life isn't all that linear. Kevin is exploring the Zettelkasten method. It is about connecting the dots and embracing the journey, which is not a direct path to completing the picture. It's more of a system where all dots are connected. During these times of transition and deciding which "rabbit" to chase, Kevin understands he may have to give space for one to take the lead and the other to percolate. It's like he and Ann are doing with writing their books. Write one at a time and let the other ideas percolate. The time will come for them to take the lead, just like the time will come for your goals and dreams to take the lead, one idea at a time because if you chase two rabbits, two books, two businesses, both may get away.

It doesn't mean you won't accept things that don't pay or that you won't volunteer your time or your services. It just means it's important to know where you are and how to align all the choices. Just because one path opens up doesn't mean that the other is closed off. It just means that if it's truly meant for you, it will present itself again and you will make it happen.

So, when Kevin is facing two major things he wants to do, he asks himself the tough questions and listens to the answer and whether or not it's *hell no* or a *hell yeah*.

Two Businesses. Choosing the Priority and Setting Goals.

Ann knew she wanted and would someday have her own business. Throughout the summers and periodically during the school year, from fifth grade until high school graduation, she worked with her dad in his currency exchange and license plate business. Modeling a strong work ethic and customer focus, her dad instilled in her some of the core values she carries to this day in her own businesses.

Being a life-long learner and feeling as if there's always room to elevate knowledge and skills, Ann began facilitating professional-development workshops. Several years later she was introduced to the world of coaching and became a credentialed coach where she partners with leaders and teams in figuring out what their priorities and goals are for the future, developing an action plan with them, and helping them figure out what they are willing and able to commit to in order to accomplish their goals. Hence, she created her coaching and training business, The Wright Coaching and Training Solutions.

In the meantime, she also had the opportunity to become a Norwex consultant where she shared how people could clean without chemicals in a more environmentally friendly way using Norwex's high-quality microfiber and water. The opportunity to be part of a movement and successful company was appealing. She became and still is a consultant.

However, as you know, accomplishing goals and growing a business takes time and energy. While both businesses were working, they weren't flourishing like she felt they could. It was time to make a tough choice about which business to pursue, even though she enjoyed and had a passion for each one. Chasing two rabbits, in this case two businesses, was overwhelming and needless to say, exhausting.

How did she determine where to invest her time and energy? She took time to reflect on where she was and looked forward to five years down the road where she wanted to be. She used her *Seven-Steps to Balance* process and determined her priority was to expand her coaching and training business as that's where she could make the biggest impact—partnering with people to support them in being who they wanted to be and accomplish in life what they wanted to accomplish.

Does she still serve her Norwex customers? Absolutely. She just isn't hosting parties or seeking out new business at the moment.

Did she make the "right" decision on which rabbit to chase? Yes. Once she began to invest more time in her coaching and training, her goal of working with even more people and organizations materialized.

She let go of one business to focus on one business.

It was hard. It was challenging. It was freeing.

Choosing priorities and what to focus on first isn't something that goes away. She then had to make choices when deciding on which new ideas and areas of the business she needed to focus on to continue reaching her dreams. She took a step back to take two forwards.

She made a conscious decision and commitment to herself. Before she "chased" any additional certifications or accepted any major volunteer positions, she was going to finish this book. Maybe people would read it. Maybe they wouldn't. But she would finish and publish the first book, then launch her podcast, and write the second book with Noah.

"F.O.O.C.U.S. — Focus On One Course Until Successful"

Benjamin J. Harvey

Lessons Learned

- There's not a right or wrong answer per se. There may, however, be a right or wrong answer for *you*.

- If it's important, go for it. If not, stop and change direction. You can always revisit the situation.

- Make time to "chase" dreams and make them a reality. Each has its own season. You can always go back and work on the one who you thought got away.

- It's important to figure out which rabbit to chase when.

- There are seasons in our lives. People come and go in and out of our lives just like ideas and goals. Kevin and Ann said that there are seasons in life and it's okay if some of our rabbits get away. Maybe some of them need to get away. Maybe we need to let go of some, at least for the time being.

- You have ideas so you have choices. Consider what is important and make a choice.

- Just because you say no today does not mean it's no forever. And when you say no to one thing, you say yes to another.

- Trust yourself.

- Set your goal. Determine your action steps and timeline. Then do it. Evaluate the results. Celebrate milestones.

- You don't have to change anything, but if you want a different result you need to change something.

"Failing to plan is planning to fail."

Benjamin Franklin

My Strengths

- I encourage you to ask yourself, "is what you're chasing in alignment with what is important to you?"

- I give you choices and ideas.

Your Strengths (List the strengths you see in yourself when it comes to choosing priorities and setting goals.)

Strategies: Choose the one(s) which will best serve you.

- Stay true to your values and what's important to you in each season of life.

- Stop. Assess your goals. Write down your priorities. They might be family, school, work, a book, a certification, a podcast, a webinar, a new hobby, or a plethora of other things important to you. There are not necessarily any right answers—yet there are answers that are right for you.

- Have a conversation with your future self. What advice would your future, five-years-older-and-wiser self, give to you? Then write a letter to yourself, from your future self—one, five, ten years down the road. Write the letter as if you have already achieved one or both goals. Which one gives you the biggest goosebumps? What will you be celebrating at the end of the year?

- Evaluate to determine if your hopes and dreams are in alignment with your values and what you say are your priorities in life. Here are some questions you may want to ask yourself. Answer the ones most important to you.

    - Are my dreams and goals in alignment with my values and priorities at the time and in the future?

    - What keeps me up at night?

    - What dreams and goals give me goosebumps?

    - How much time can I invest in this?

    - What are my long-term goals?

    - What other commitments do I have?

    - Is this the right time for this goal?

    - Is it the right goal for me?

    - What's of interest to me right now?

    - What resources do I have and/or need?

    - How much bandwidth or capacity do I have right now?

    - Do I have the right mindset?

    - Do I have the time?

    - How does it feel when I think about working on each goal? Exciting? Stressful? (Though just because it's stressful doesn't mean you shouldn't pursue it.)

    - Why am I avoiding progressing on one or both big goals?

    - Am I fearful of failure or am I afraid of the success it may bring, which brings a higher level of expectations?

    - Are my hopes and dreams in alignment with my values and what I say are my priorities in life? (Your answer(s) will give you clarity, focus, and peace of mind.)

- Make time to reflect on what is important to you.

- Develop a timeline. What can you reasonably accomplish in a particular time period?

- Talk to people you trust. Ask for their opinion. Do not ask them what you should do. It's not fair to place that responsibility on them. You are responsible for your own life, happiness, and choices. You have to live with the consequences of your decisions, both positive and negative.

- Find an accountability partner—someone who will support you and challenge you with meeting your timeframe for your project. Be sure the person is not someone who will criticize you or say—"I told you so," but someone who will support you and ask tough questions with kindness.

- Conduct research if needed.

- Seek out more education or experience to achieve your goal.

- Do things in phases. Mitch Matthews, a highly successful entrepreneur, coach, writer, and podcaster, teaches us to do things in phases.

- Make a commitment to yourself and a project. Work on it for a certain amount of time and then decide if you want to continue.

- Meditate and sit in silence (Kevin).

- Make the decision on what to focus on first.

- Gather all the facts.

- Make a list of pros and cons for each goal. Sometimes the length of the list will provide clarity. Remember, it's not always the length of each list, but the essence of what is written.
  - What will it take to accomplish your goal(s)?
  - How will you feel when you achieve it?
  - How will you feel if you don't?
- Weigh the importance of each goal. On a scale of 1–10 (10 being the most important) how important is each goal to you currently? Where are you on the excitement scale of each goal or project?
- Make and take time to write your goals and values at the end of this chapter. Remember, just because you say no to something today doesn't mean it's no forever—it means no not right now. Here's the good news—it means *yes* to something else and what's important now. Companies decide on priorities all the time. They decide which products or services to launch based on capacity. What's your capacity? Ann delayed working on this book because she wanted to earn her PCC (Professional Certified Coach) for coaching. She set the goal, had a deadline, and worked hard and achieved it.

When figuring out what you want to work on and how to prioritize your time feel free to use the **The Windshield and the Rearview Mirror** (Life/work balance) form at the end of the book or go to Ann's website to access a free copy of it. www.annwrightsolutions.com

Your Reflection

Reflection Questions: Answer here or in a separate journal.

1. Do I have a dream that got away? Or did it just take a vacation and now it's time to revisit it and go after it?

2. Which rabbit do I want to tackle first?

3. How important is this goal?

4. Do I have the resources I need to achieve my goal? If not, what do I need?

Your Biggest Take-Away(s) Regarding Choosing Priorities and Setting Goals

Your Action Plan

Here is an example of what your action plan may look like. Remember it's your plan not mine, this is only an example to support you in getting started. Choose the action which will support you in moving forward. There is space for you to write your personal plan of action at the end of the example.

1. *Goal: Determine 2024 business priorities and goals including action steps and timelines for each.*

2. *Action: Set aside one or two days in July to plan my business goals and priorities for 2024. List each in my calendar with dates and times I will work on them.*

3. *Who will support me? My husband.*

4. *Date to begin: May 1, Put dates on calendar. July 17 and 18 develop plan for 2024.*

5. *How will I know I made progress? By the end of the day on July 18, I will have a plan for 2024, listing business priorities with action steps and timeline for 2024.*

Your Turn: Answer here or in a separate journal.

1. Goal:

2. Action:

3. Who can support you?

4. Date to begin:

5. How will you know you made progress?

It takes time, energy, and hard work to move forward with your goals and it's worth it. As quickly as I move, the next member of the team is going to lend a hand in learning the importance of slowing down.

Additional Resources

- *Start with your Why* by Simon Sinek.
- *Find Your Why* by Simon Sinek.
- *BookFactory Universal Note Taking System* (Cornell Notes) (Note Taking Notebook).
- *Digital Zettelkasten: Principles, Methods, & Examples* by David Kadavy.
- *Powerful* by Patti McCord.

The Sloth
Slowing Down

"Cut yourself some slack without slacking off."

Ann Wright

Ever feel as if you are just not motivated enough and are moving slower than normal? You know, the times when you feel lazy, and yet the reality is, you may be overwhelmed. Ann's husband looks at her with the most perplexed expression when she asks him if he thinks she's lazy, and says, "What are you talking about? You are *not* lazy—you just have too much going on at the moment."

Some of my friends think I'm lazy but my friends, the geese, recognize that I help everyone learn it's important to slow down and take their time to do things well. I'm fondly known as your sloth team member. It may seem as if I take forever to get to the destination or make a decision. You may think I'm slacking off, but I just move slower than my other teammates. Some might look at me as a detriment. Others look at me as an asset. So, when you're tired and feel lazy and not moving as fast as you think you "should" be, maybe it's your body's way of saying, you're not lazy, you just need to slow down.

Do you ever ask yourself what in the world is causing you to feel this way? Ann does. During the pandemic, some attributed it to being home too much and being overwhelmed with the news. There was so much change and isolation! I noticed a lot of people moved slower than they normally did. However, what about when there isn't a pandemic?

Slowing down doesn't mean a lack of progress. It may mean you're taking time to rethink things or ask yourself or your peers those tough questions. Am I doing the right thing? Are we forging ahead without doing due diligence in researching our product?

Ann used to hate it when I showed up, but not anymore. I, like my other friends, have many qualities to support her. I help remind her to slow down, take time to consider and contemplate the possibilities and next steps in the journey.

I gave her and, and I give you, "permission" to pause and consider the priorities at the moment and what the future possibilities are.

I can be methodical. What some may view as slow, others may see as being systematic. It's tough to be excited about a project or idea and have me take over and run interference; however, I just want everyone to think everything through before they proceed. I also want things done right and sometimes if you go too fast you miss some of the important details. The other advantage of taking things a little slower is you have more of a chance to get it right the first time and enjoy the journey along the way instead of rushing through things just to check them off your list.

Ann enjoys a few TV programs, but have you ever let yourself get distracted with TV shows when in your heart you know you want something else? She has, then asks herself, why am I letting myself get distracted? Then when the sloth and the snake team up, distractions can dominate or sidetrack, and she can really be in trouble.

Once you understand me, you can capitalize on what I offer you, and what I can offer your team members. Ann has taught at the college level for over 20 years. The silent, and sometimes not so silent, groans when team projects are assigned echo throughout the room or in the comments in her online classes. Students are not fans of team projects. Why? Because there are plenty of projects in the classroom and in the business world when I show up in one of your team members. You know the person who, in your opinion, doesn't pull their weight or is slow to begin their part of the assignment. If everyone talked about expectations, timelines, and how each other worked, the team might realize the importance of beginning sooner and give everyone the chance to ask questions as well as collaborate on the entire project.

I think it's easy to jump to conclusions. Many times, there are things going on with people that don't necessarily show up on the outside. Why does it take some people longer to work on or finish things than others? I have found some of the following reasons people may take more time than some think is needed to do things.

- Being overwhelmed
- Feeling intimidated.
- Just being tired.
- Needing extra time to think things through before making a decision.
- Not being certain how to proceed.
- Don't know where to begin.
- Don't want to do it.
- Feeling as if there are other priorities.
- Naturally, just needing more time to complete a project—which is perfectly okay.

If we aren't careful, we can misinterpret someone or ourselves as being lazy or slow when in reality your team member or you are taking time to contemplate all the options, ask the needed questions, and research the information needed. I encourage you to stop, get clear or remember your values and priorities, and enjoy the journey. Life and experiences are gifts, that's why we call it the present. Be mindful and stop and smell the roses, yet be watchful of the thorns.

Busy, Busy, Busy

Ann had a friend who indicated she was so busy helping everyone else with their work, which admittedly was part of her job, she had a difficult time getting her own work done during the day. This resulted in her working many hours past her normal end time. In her job, it was normal to work some nights and weekends, however, not to the extreme she was working.

Ann asked her friend a variety of questions, gave her time and space to reflect on the organization and her daily routines, and listened as she described what a normal day consisted of.

Her friend allowed herself to be constantly interrupted by her team and herself. She hopped from one project to the next without finishing an activity, as well as checked every email and text alert in real time. It should be noted that there are times when emails need to be checked immediately based on the job and project, yet this isn't the case in every job and every day all day long.

Ann listened to her friend as she talked through when she was most productive, the needs of her team, and how she might be able to be more efficient with her time. Her friend came up with several ideas and landed on setting some boundaries with her team. She decided to work on major projects in the morning when she was most productive, using time blocks, so she had a dedicated period of time to get her own projects finished in a timely manner. She also set aside 'office hours' so her team could meet with her as needed. After slowing down to figure things out, she became more efficient and productive with her time.

She had the answers—she just hadn't discovered them—yet.

Yet is one of Ann's favorite words because it implies she will eventually figure things out.

Noah and the AP Classes. Slowing down and taking time to listen to what is and isn't said. Asking powerful questions—discovering practical solutions: The cat and the sloth work together.

Noah was a multi-sport athlete all four years of high school. During his junior and senior year he took multiple AP classes. He decided to take the AP tests at the end of his senior year, so they counted toward his college degree.

At breakfast one morning, during track season on a late-start Wednesday, Ann asked him when the study reviews were for the AP tests. He shared the dates and times and indicated he may or may not attend, and if he did, he might only stay for half of the time. Ann thought that seemed odd, as she knew grades were important to him. She asked him how important it was to him to pass the exams.

He said, "Very."

She asked if he thought the study reviews might help.

He said, "Yes."

Ann asked if there was a reason he only planned to stay for half the time if he went at all.

As she listened to him talk, he shared that track practice ended at 5:15/5:30. Study sessions and reviews began at 6:00 and ended at 8:00. He shared his concerns about being hungry and not being able to concentrate as well as being too tired to do other homework after the reviews. They talked. Ann asked what she could do to make it possible for him to attend the study sessions if he wanted to. He shared that if something was ready for him to eat at 5:30 he could get home, eat, and get back for the reviews by 6:00. Ann left it up to him whether he stayed the entire time.

Decision made. Food would be ready. Noah would eat quickly and attend the review sessions. His choice.

He attended all of the review sessions and stayed the entire time.

Simon Sinek says leaders should learn to speak last—much easier said than done. Whether you're a parent, a peer, or a supervisor, there is a time to tell and a time to ask. There is a time to let people weigh the alternatives and make their own decisions. Each has its place and is of equal importance. The challenge is figuring out when to ask and when to tell.

The cat and I worked together, each giving Ann and Noah what they needed. Each slowing down. Digging deep. Asking questions. Listening to the other person to both what was and wasn't said. People usually have the answer, they just may not have discovered it—yet.

Lessons Learned

- It's okay to slow down and reflect.
- Sometimes it takes a little longer to bring the quality you want to your work.
- It's about progress, not perfection.
- Keep moving forward.

"Strive for excellence, not perfection."

Unknown

My Strengths

- I help you take time to reflect.
- I encourage you to make time to discover what inspires you as well as your team members.

Your Strengths (List the strengths you see in yourself when it comes to being able to slow down when needed.)

Strategies: Choose the one(s) which will best serve you.

- Move at the rate that makes sense for you and for the project.
- Take time to think and plan.
- Go somewhere that provides you space to think without distractions.
- **Ask for help.** If you're moving slowly because you don't know what to do or where to start, ask someone you trust to help you. It doesn't mean they're going to do it for you, it just means they can support you in either getting started or helping you talk through it.

Your Reflection

Reflection Questions: Answer here or in a separate journal.

1. When and in what circumstances have you felt the need to slow down?

2. What are some of the advantages gained when you take the time to slow down?

Your Biggest Take-away(s) Regarding Slowing Down

Your Action Plan

Here is an example of what your action plan may look like. Remember it's your plan not mine, this is only an example to support you in getting started. Choose the action which will support you in moving forward. There is space for you to write your personal plan of action at the end of the example.

1. *Goal: Give myself at least 24 hours before I make a decision to commit to a new volunteer position.*

2. *Action: As much as I love being a volunteer, the time has come to step back, and determine where I want to invest my time. I will thank the person who invites me to do something and share with them that I need to think about whether or not I am able to give the position the time and attention it needs. I will then share with them within a day or two if I will be able to take the position. I am also going to take time to list the different organizations and causes in which I am most interested and figure out how I can support them in time and donations.*

3. *Who will support me? I need to be accountable to myself. My husband can also support me in this.*

4. *Date: The next time I'm asked to take on a volunteer position. In December of each year, I will take time to evaluate where I am investing my time and where I want to invest time in the coming year. Decisions will be made by 12/31 of each year.*

5. *How will I know I'm making progress? I will monitor if I'm taking time to consider the invitation. I will review where I volunteer each year and where my monetary donations are invested each year and compare them with where I said I wanted to volunteer the prior year.*

"For fast-acting relief try slowing down."

Lily Tomlin

Your Turn: Answer here or in a separate journal.

1. Goal:

2. Action:

3. Who can support you?

4. Date to begin:

5. How will you know you made progress?

Can you see the importance of taking a few minutes to slow down and how by slowing down you may actually be able to save time in the long run? Admittedly the next team member may be challenging to read about. Ann has to take a deep breath when leading the snake who adds value even if at first it doesn't feel like it.

Additional Resources

- Simon Sinek's TEDxs.
- Books
- *The Advice Trap* by Michael Bungay Stanier.
- "The Advice Monster" TED Talk by Michael Bungay Stanier.

The Snake

Comparison, Fear, and Self-doubt

"Fear kills more dreams than failure ever will."

Suzy Kassem

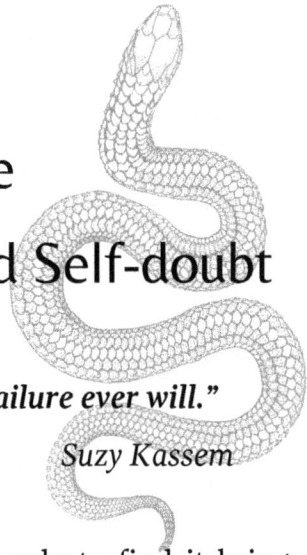

*E*ver compare yourself to others only to find it brings despair? Maybe a dose of self-doubt and a healthy cup of fear accompanied with comparison? These "gifts" are from me. Don't worry, my chapter isn't full of doom and gloom. It's actually about facing these three concepts head-on and figuring out how to work with them—because if you don't, they can and will sabotage your success. I know you know what's coming—you can't change what you don't acknowledge. Besides, who wants to talk about any of them? Not most people. You might even wonder how could these gifts of mine possibly help you? They can't if you let them take the lead. And if you ignore them and leave them all alone, they win. Just like the elephant, if you don't talk about them, they just get bigger and bigger.

Like some of the other members of the team, I didn't expect to be included in the group, let alone be in this book about leadership. Truth—they almost left me out. But staying true to their word, the geese knew I brought some kind of value to the team, even though most people aren't all that fond of me. Ann isn't. She, like most people, would like to forget about me, but I'm going to be there no matter how hard you try to ignore me, so you may as well decide how to lead me within yourself so you can support others when I show

189

up in them. When you face your challenges and figure out how to address them, you can and will conquer them and be stronger for it.

I am the team member who Ann refers to as the snake.

The geese acknowledge that I am part of the team, regardless of whether people like me or what I have to say. Most people, in general and experienced and inexperienced leaders, meet me at some point in their lives. They have doubts and fears, and compare themselves to others. By facing me head on, you can take steps to conquer your fears, build your self-confidence, and be better prepared to move forward toward your goals. Once you can manage yourself, you will be in a better position to help others overcome fear and self-doubt and stop, or at least reduce, the time they spend comparing themselves to others, therefore helping them build their self-confidence.

Comparison, fear, and self-doubt can lead to a lack of confidence. In order to address them, I'm the catalyst that propels you to question aspects of your life and decisions. By encouraging you to look at all aspects, you can stay on the same path, wiser and more prepared, or decide to take a different viewpoint or path because I've encouraged you to stop and think about things. If you face them head on, you can work to figure out how to overcome the challenges they bring.

Comparison, fear, and self-doubt may feel gigantic, yet in reality they are not as big as they would like you to think. People give them way too much power. Do you give them too much power in your life? Do you let them grow and become bigger than they are by the stories you tell yourself or the rabbit holes you let yourself go down? Sorry, my rabbit friend. You can overcome things that are twice your size. Heck, I eat things that are more than twice my size!

I bring up the emotions, then it's up to you to ask the questions and determine if your fears are real or the fictitious voice working to make space in your thoughts causing you to be afraid. Is it a story you told yourself? Is it something somebody said? An unpleasant experience? A mistake made? Lack of knowledge? What's important is you take time to address the issues and figure out what action(s) you are willing to take to lead yourself to meet them head on and overcome them.

I am the master of disguise. I have coats of many colors. I also shed my skin, so comparison, fear, and self-doubt have plenty of opportunities to show up, be fed and shed. However, when I'm finished with one, I just move on to the next. You might be thinking, wouldn't it be better if you just got rid of me? I don't know. That's up to you. Many people are afraid of snakes. Ann is. They creep her out. They quietly slither along, mostly going unnoticed until you almost step on them, and then suddenly, they're there, like comparison, fear, and self-doubt. Just like some snakes are poisonous, some thoughts are, too. Your inner thoughts can fuel and poison your success if you let them.

Some snakes, like the San Francisco garter snake, with bright turquoise, deep coral, and black stripes, are considered among the most beautiful snakes in the world, yet despite their beauty, and lack of danger to humans, can still cause angst. How can comparison, fear, and self-doubt have any beauty? They can create space and inspire you to pause and ponder all those thoughts rolling around in your head as well as examine what's at the root of each and causing all the angst. Prepare and plan for them. If they're valid, meet them head on and conquer. If they never happen, you were prepared. If they happen, you will be prepared. Hope for the best, plan for the worst. Don't dwell on it. Pivot if needed. Proceed with your plan.

> *"We won't be distracted by comparison if we are captivated with purpose."*
>
> *Bob Goff*

Comparison—Do you wonder why people compare themselves to others? Why do you compare yourself to others? Comparison leads to despair if you let it. Social media has made my job so much easier for me. You know the drill. Everyone else's life is so much more fun, more successful, more this, more that, than yours. But is it? Are you really comparing apples to apples when you compare yourself with others? It's convenient to see what the celebrities are doing as well as what many people you know are doing. Posts about houses, awards, and trips can cause you to question how your own life stacks up. Can you be happy for others? Absolutely. It's great to celebrate their wins. Sometimes it's easier to be happy for others when things are going well in your own life. It's also possible to be happy for others and still question what's going on in your life.

Even if you feel you're on Chapter Twenty, you're writing a different book than someone else. It's your book. It's your life. It's your journey. We all get to where we're going, taking different paths. Life really is a journey and not a destination. 'Cause I don't know about you, but just when I think I've arrived, there's somewhere else I want to go. You may wonder what the heck the upside is, or is there an upside to comparison? You bet there is, it can cause you to think about what it is someone has or has accomplished and ask yourself, "Is this something to which I really want to aspire," or is the squirrel enticing you to follow the next shiny object, taking your focus off your own goal?

The grass isn't always greener on the other side; it's just a different shade of green. There are people looking at your yard and thinking your grass is greener than theirs. Yours isn't greener, it's just a different color green. By the way, if you are truly interested in aspiring to work toward a similar goal that someone has, then work toward it. Ann is working toward being a successful author. She also looks forward to celebrating and achieving her milestone in publishing her first book. If you're reading this, she accomplished it and believe me, she fell into the trap of comparison, which didn't serve her well in the beginning.

She loves the quote by Nido Qubein, "*Winners* compare their achievements with their goals."

This is one she is working to remember when I sneak up on her. Look at your goals and what you've achieved, not only the end result but also what you've learned and how much you've grown on the journey in accomplishing your goals.

> *"Don't compare your chapter one to someone else's chapter twenty."*
>
> *Unknown*

Fear—It can be paralyzing. It can be poisonous. It can protect you. It's like the lights and sounds at a railroad crossing that cause you to stop and let the train pass before you move on. In this case the warning lights and fear, or knowledge of the fast-approaching train, protect you from moving into the path of the oncoming train. It can cause you to look for danger ahead. I'm like the yellow light or the road sign, which encourages you to stop, look, listen, think, and then proceed with caution as you move into taking action to accomplish your goals.

For example: what are you really afraid of? Is what you're telling yourself true? Does it have merit? Does it serve you? Or are you allowing comparison, an imagined fear, and self-doubt to control you? Have you examined the consequences and prepared for them? Do you need more knowledge, or do you need or have a backup plan? Is this the path you need and want to take?

You may decide to proceed on the path in front of you and if it doesn't work out—you just learned what doesn't work so you can take the next path, which may lead to what you do want. It took Thomas Edison and his team thousands of attempts to invent the electric light bulb.

Some have asked, "Are you more afraid of success or failure?" No one likes to fail, yet we all do at some point, many times, multiple times. If you don't fail, you're probably not trying enough new things. Think about how much you learn from your so-called failures. I've heard it said, "it's only a failure if you fail to learn from it." How much more would you, as well as kids, learn if you asked yourself, what did I learn from this or what will I do differently next time? I may not be as toxic as you think—it's all in perspective.

And think of an epic fail as an Epic F.A.I.L.—First Attempt In Learning.

Success—Do you ever wonder how anyone could be fearful of success? It's kind of like what Marianne Williamson said in her quote, "Our greatest fear is not that we are inadequate.

It is that we are powerful beyond measure. It is our light, and not our darkness, that frightens us."

Once you're successful, do you feel people or maybe you have even higher expectations of and for you? Ann wants everyone to be as successful as they want and are able. Take a moment and define what success is for you. Don't let others define it for you. Different people not only define success in different ways, it's also different for people based on their capabilities.

Self-doubt—How do you feel when doubt creeps in? Most people who hear those self-doubts want to turn around and run the other way, ignore them, or dwell on them. I'm not certain which is worse. I mean, why would you want to put yourself out there and risk being ridiculed by others? What if you make a mistake or say the wrong thing? Ann has students doubt their ability to make polished presentations or interview well. She encourages them to ask themselves hard questions, like have they done the work to develop a good presentation and practice it? Besides, they are only going to get better with practice.

Are you sabotaging your own success? Is your peer, who appears to be the snake, trying to make you look bad, or is it your imagination? Maybe the feedback is meant to help you do what you need to do to be successful. Maybe the person has your best interest at heart and wants to be sure you have looked at as many of the angles as possible.

What causes you to doubt yourself when you have a thought, an idea, or a project you're working on and excited about and then suddenly you wonder if you should share the thought or work toward the goal? This isn't about not wanting to do something, it could be something you really want to accomplish; however, for various reasons, an incident in your past, something someone said that's stuck in your head, or lack of knowledge or experience makes you question whether this goal can become a reality. Look at this book! Ann finished it. You can finish yours, too!

There are all kinds of books on self-doubt and the imposter syndrome, so I'm not going to go into depth. I just want you to know that most have doubts at some point in their life. Ann's snake shows up. It might be when writing a book, working on her coaching practice and workshops, parenting, being a wife. Her self-doubt was grounded more in fear than anything. With the book, she felt she had something to share, but what if she couldn't get what was in her head and heart on paper, so it made sense? She didn't want to preach—she wanted to partner. I caused her to ask herself tough questions and overcome self-doubt. I even helped her write from an entirely unique point of view because of causing her to pause, ponder, pivot, and proceed.

Like me, you can shed your "skin" and adopt a new way of thinking about comparison, fear, and self-doubt while staying true to your core values and who you are. It is up to you to determine who you want to be. Underneath the exterior are your thoughts and core values, which will determine your actions, and ultimately set the course you decide to take to accomplish your goals. Unless you take the time to examine your inside, the outside may not matter as much.

"Never let self-doubt hold you captive."

Roy Bennett

Ann's Presentation—The Comparison

Years ago, Ann was presenting at a conference. She was excited and confident in what she had prepared to share during her workshop. After attending one of the other speaker's workshops, I showed up with, you guessed it, the *Trifecta; The Big Three:* comparison, fear, and self-doubt. Those are a lot of things to experience at the same time and on the same day as a presentation. Ann, in awe, marveled at how another speaker presented—she was so calm, cool, and confident. She stuck to her script and read her presentation without coming across as if she were reading it.

You can imagine the self-doubt and comparison she felt when she saw that same presenter sitting in the front row of her presentation. Yikes. Yep, all those voices were swirling around at the same time: "Am I going to be as good as the other speaker? Will people think I know what I'm talking about? What will that speaker think?"

The inner dialogue went on and on.

She quickly composed her thoughts and instead of allowing me to take over, she relied on her eagle. The one with confidence and determination to deliver the best presentation possible to the audience because they deserved her best. She reminded herself she knew her topic, had prepared and practiced, and most importantly stayed true to delivering the material in her own style—that of a conversation.

After the presentation, that same speaker walked up to Ann and shared, "I wish I could present like you, using more intuition, spontaneity, and in more of a conversational style."

Ann thanked her, smiled, and laughed as she shared with her, "I was thinking after attending your presentation I wish I could be more like you—poised and scripted without sounding scripted."

Both laughed and realized each was equally qualified and effective because they stayed true to themselves, capitalizing on their own unique style. That was the day Ann realized it's better to be the best version of yourself than to be somebody you're not. Because it's true. Don't try to be someone else because they're already taken.

Ann's Decision to Enter a Contest—Fear and self-doubt work together, yet confidence presides.

Have you ever thought of stopping before you reached your goal? Ann wanted to enter a Modern Dickens contest where multiple authors wrote a book. It's like a progressive dinner where guests travel from one house to another, enjoying a different course for a meal at each house. The Modern Dickens contest comprised a variety of authors writing a chapter for a book that was built on the prior chapter. The same person wrote the first and last chapter. A different author wrote each chapter in between.

This idea intrigued Ann. She decided to write chapter seven and submit it to be included in the book. Comparison, fear, and self-doubt showed up in force! She worked herself into a tizzy with stories in her head—what if the selection committee didn't like what she wrote? What if it's not good enough? What if her submission didn't get chosen? What if? What if? What if? It was mind-boggling.

So, she asked herself, what's the worst that could happen? Her chapter doesn't get chosen. What's the best thing? Her chapter is chosen. Would she let fear be her guide and not try? No, like the butterfly she kept writing and editing, transforming her chapter into something she was proud to submit. Minutes before it was due, she hit the submit button. Done! Out of her hands and into the hands of the selection committee.

Life goes on. A couple weeks later, she received an email informing her that her chapter had been selected as the next chapter, Chapter Seven. What if Ann had stopped writing and didn't submit a chapter for that Dickens novel because of fear? She would never have had the chance to cry. Tears of joy. Tears of relief. Tears of fear because now her friends might also read what she wrote. It really is a vicious cycle, which she began with questions and, well, you get the picture. My place is safe on the team.

A Decision Gets Questioned—To Continue or Start Over: Self-doubt—What do you do when someone questions a decision you make?

Years ago, Ann had the honor of serving as Regional Director of Region 7 of the Iowa Jaycees. The five Regional Directors before her worked tirelessly to build the region. Positioned to lead the region to a number one finish in the nation, many questions and judgments surrounded their Board's every move. Talk about pressure. Their goal during her year as Regional Director—Lead their Region to finish as the number one region in America. The region had seven districts, over 25 chapters, and at the time, over 1700 members. Their Region would eventually finish the year with 29 chapters and over 2,500 members.

Questioned about a decision she and one of her district directors made, self-doubt set in for a brief time. They had decided to let a chapter close. She asked herself if the decision to close a chapter and begin a new one in the same town was self-centered, or in the best interest of all involved. You see, you earned more "points" for beginning a new chapter rather than re-activating a current one.

Questions whirled around for several weeks. Do they let the chapter fold? Do they work to recruit enough members to maintain the chapter's viability? Do they start over with new and enthusiastic members? What impact would the handful of current members, who had little or no interest in remaining a chapter, have on new members recruited?

Chapters needed twenty people on their roster to maintain their status as a chapter. Some were from the mindset—recruit more members into the chapter instead of starting over. There were benefits to doing this, a major benefit being an established chapter already in existence.

It was far easier to invite members to join a chapter already in existence as opposed to one that would not exist until twenty people paid their dues. However, there was one major drawback in keeping the same chapter—it had baggage, as well as members who were tired and didn't want to be there. Attitudes can poison or inspire others, whether purposely or subconsciously. Did they want to risk new members being poisoned by the negativity and exhaustion of the existing members?

In the end, it was ultimately Ann's decision, which she knew would draw criticism no matter what she decided.

What to do? Believing in second chances and fresh starts, and after much thought, discussion, and prayer, she decided to let the chapter fold and start a new chapter. It wasn't about points. It wasn't about her. It was about what would be best for the new members and the community. With the decision made, she received a phone call from someone she respected, which made the question even more challenging.

The State Membership Vice President and her friend asked, "Why start a new chapter and not save the chapter at hand? Are you sure that's the right decision?"

Ann took a breath because she knew this question would come at some point in time. She just didn't know from whom.

She had given a great deal of thought to how she would answer this question, and this is what she shared.

"Honestly, I don't know whether it's the right decision or not. However, what I do know, believe and am sure of is this— it's the best decision at this time based on all the information I have. I have talked to people, looked at the data available, looked at the pros and cons and believe this is what's best for the people of the community. It's time for a fresh start."

The person on the other end of the phone paused before commenting, "Okay, that's really all anyone could ask for and that's good enough for me."

At the time, Ann felt she was being questioned. Ann realized later, her friend was questioning her to gain a deeper understanding of the reason the decision was made, not the decision itself. Looking back, it's clear the question was asked with the best of intentions.

Joe Returns to School

Joe, a friend and fellow coach, returned to school to earn a second master's degree after leaving a company where he was a Senior Project Manager, where he wrote proposals and scripts, as well as did some programming and graphic manipulation. He was truly a "Joe of all trades."

Excited to begin his new career, he interviewed for a teaching position at a middle school, where he completed his student teaching. He got the job! Eight weeks into it, he realized it was not a good fit, so he resigned the position, knowing it could be detrimental to his career. Fear and self-doubt set in. Did he make the right decision to change careers? Would he find something he enjoyed? My strength encouraged him to ask himself great questions. Being honest with himself and staying true to what he valued and knowing what he wanted in life he didn't let me stop him. He persevered and let the tortoise work with me and kept going.

Are you curious about how things turned out? Joe was curious how everything would turn out, too.

Did resigning leave a negative mark on his career? No. He ended up substituting at the same school district from which he resigned. The next school year, he landed a long-term sub position for a teacher on maternity leave. As he neared the end of that time, he was asked to apply for a literacy position. He didn't get that job because his mentor did. However, he got the teaching job, which became available when his mentor got promoted.

What did he learn? He had the courage and patience and took time to figure out what went well. He evaluated the good, the bad, and the ugly. To his surprise, it turned out to be better than he had hoped. Don't quit just because one experience didn't go your way. Just because it's a poor fit doesn't mean you're not good at what you do. Keep searching for what you want. Joe persevered and discovered he really enjoys working with high school students.

What's he doing now? He is teaching English at a high school, facilitating improv workshops, coaching, and encouraging others to follow their dreams.

"Uninstall self-doubt from your mind."

Anonymous

Lessons Learned

- You are enough.

- Don't compare your Chapter 1 to someone else's Chapter 20. It's a dream killer. Figure out what it is you admire about them or what they're doing and decide if it's something you want to work on or not. If it is, then work to develop the knowledge and skills needed to accomplish your own goals, not someone else's. If it's not something that's important to you, let it go.

- Evaluate fear. Fears come and go. Are your fears substantiated in facts or myths to which you subscribe based on things said by those who don't care about you or your own self-sabotages?

- There is a difference between asking a question and questioning. Asking a question is just that—asking for a deeper understanding of yourself or others. Questioning can cause doubt. You wonder if others believe you. Determine the intent behind the question—are you asking or being asked the question for a deeper understanding, to protect you and to be better prepared for what is about to come? Instead of allowing your inner critic or snake to taunt you, remind yourself to examine intent.

- Assume positive Intent.

- Comparison, fear and self-doubt can be liars—they can rob you of your happiness and full potential, take over your life, paralyze your progress *if* you allow them to. They can take your breath away and leave you drowning in a sea of self-doubt. *However, they can also challenge you and make you stronger.*

- You have what you need, or you can develop the skills needed to be who and what you want to be.

- Lean on your peers.

My Strengths

- I bring to the surface your fears and work together with the cat to support you in asking yourself tough questions about what you can do to discover the reasons you compare yourself to others, what it is you're really fearful of, and the reasons you doubt yourself.

- I cause you to examine whether or not what another person is doing or what they have is really important to you or do you just think you want it because someone else has it?

- I encourage you to face your fears head-on.

Your Strengths (List the strengths you see in yourself when it comes to recognizing when comparison, fear, and self-doubt emerge.)

Strategies: Choose the one(s) which will best serve you.

- Write about a time when you experienced fear, self-doubt, and/or compared yourself to others. What did you do to overcome the emotions?

- Write about a time you were confident and moved forward on a project when you were fearful but forged ahead anyway. What caused you to move forward?

- Ask yourself the hard questions so you can lead the snake instead of him leading you.
    - How do I handle a toxic team member?
    - Is he a distraction or a deterrent?
    - Is my snake cause for pause?
    - Is it in my best interest?
    - Is someone trying to trip me up?
    - Am I tripping myself up?
    - Is what I'm doubting real or fiction?
    - What are the obstacles I need to overcome?
    - Is this true or just my own self-doubt?
- Find resources to help you.
- Hope for the best, prepare for the worst.
- Plan for the "what if."
- Consciously lead and control your own thoughts.
- Talk to someone about what you're feeling.
- Ask for help if you need it.
- Consciously suggest other ways to think about things.
- Lean on your friends and support system. Determine who the people are who you can count on to listen to you. Who are your cheerleaders? Text them. Call them. Talk to them.
- Pray—Ann prays for help with her challenges. She used to pray for certain things, well, truth be told she still does sometimes. But she's working hard to pray for whatever God knows she needs. That is not easy. If you don't choose prayer, that's perfectly OK. Different things work for different people.

- Have a book, or song you turn to for inspiration. Ann loves books.

- Surround yourself with things that have meaning and purpose, for example: pictures, quotes, books. Choose what works for you.

- Mind maps can be helpful not only for books, but for papers, projects, just about anything—even for mapping out your fears, their causes, and what you will do to overcome them.

- Consciously stop comparing yourself to others. Instead compare where you are to where you want to be. Then make a plan on what you need to do to accomplish your goal(s) and are willing and able to do.

Your Reflection

Reflection Questions: Answer here or in a separate journal.

1. What do I gain or lose when I compare myself to others?

2. When do comparison, fear, or self-doubt show up in my life? What can I do to overcome each as I move forward?

3. Is it failure or success I fear and why?

4. What are some of my greatest fears? (For example, not strong enough, not worthy, not loveable, not good enough, not confident? Not funny?) The list can go on and on.

5. Am I my own worst enemy when it comes to comparison, fear, self-doubt?

6. If it weren't for fear, what would I do?

Your Biggest Take-away(s) Regarding Comparison, Fear, and Self-doubt

Your Action Plan

Here is an example of what your action plan may look like. Remember it's your plan not mine, this is only an example to support you in getting started. Choose the action which will support you in moving forward. There is space for you to write your personal plan of action at the end of the example.

1. *Goal: To reduce self-doubt.*

2. *Action: Call one of my friends and talk things over with them. If I have doubts about my ability, etc., they will ask me hard questions and will talk through the reasons self-doubt has surfaced. I'd like to eliminate self-doubt; however, it returns sometimes when I least expect it or when I'm trying something new. They remind me of what I can do—not what I can't.*

3. *Who will support me? I'm very fortunate. Shelley, Marci, or Cindi will support me on this.*

4. *Date: This is ongoing as I will contact them when self-doubt shows up.*

5. *How will I know I'm making progress? Recognizing when a conversation is necessary, and being honest if there is a good reason to doubt my ability, meaning I just may need to elevate my skills, or if I'm letting the imposter syndrome show up for no reason at all due to the fear of being judged.*

Your Turn: Answer here or in a separate journal.

1. Goal:
2. Action:
3. Who can support you?
4. Date to begin:
5. How will you know you made progress?

Now that we've talked about what I bring to you, let's see how distractions and interruptions can be strengths and give you cause to pause and consider what's important to work on now. My friend the squirrel is a master at this.

Additional Resources

- *The Imposter Syndrome Workbook: Exercises to Boost Your Confidence, Own Your Success, and Embrace Your Brilliance* by Athina Danilo.
- "Fear is a Liar" (song) by Zach Williams.

The Squirrel

Distractions and Interruptions

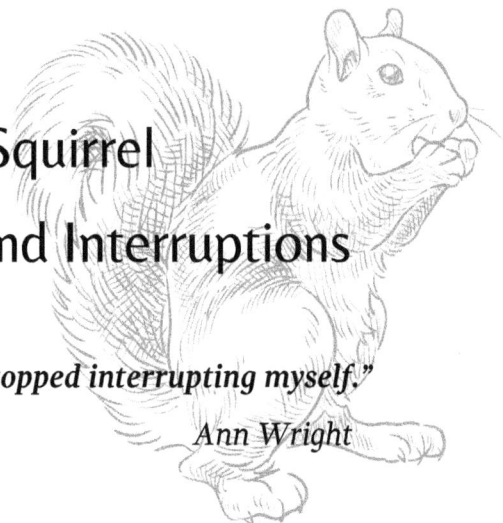

"I'd get more done if I stopped interrupting myself."

Ann Wright

When I met the geese, they just quacked and laughed at all the time I spent running all over the place because, let's face it, as a team they're focused on their goal and reaching their destination. I'm not. I have so many ideas and choices it's not funny. I can also take the long way to get to where I'm going. There are days I'm not sure what to focus on so I just keep following the next shiny object. It's fun. It's exciting. It's exhausting!

Recognize me? I figured you did. I'm the squirrel you and your friends talk about! I'm the part of you that gets super excited at the next great idea and so distracted with all the things needing done that I lose my train of thought, run from one thing to the next, and rarely make it to the priority at hand.

Leading me can be challenging because I get excited and start things and then get excited about the next shiny object or latest and greatest idea and move on before finishing the first thing or my goal. Ann can relate to this because she is challenged with the details. Loves the ideas but the details are hard, as is the follow-through because of a variety of factors—time being the main one. She knows the importance of follow-through. It's just the details and the time it takes to finish certain projects that can be challenging. Thank goodness the turtle works with me because slow and steady wins the race to finish the project.

Ann and her friends talk about me in almost every conversation. They laugh because they can all relate. I usually come up when they are going off on tangents about the projects they want to finish, and while they may all be good ones, there's only so much time in the day. They share with each other that right as they begin to focus and work on a project, just like that, another project or something on their to-do list is in sight, and they're off—scurrying from one thought or project to the next without really completing any of them. Sometimes they try to do too many things at the same time and end up not doing any of them the way they think they should be done or worse yet, they don't finish any of them in a timely manner. Can you relate?

You might be wondering, what in the world do I bring to the team? I give you choices like my rabbit co-worker does. However, I give you *many* choices and usually show up on a daily basis at work and home. I can distract you by invading your brain with emails and texts that need answering, projects requiring attention, meetings that need attending, ideas worth pursuing or exploring, laundry, paper piles to sort, stacked dishes that need washing, hence pulling you in multiple directions. The list goes on and on.

With our hybrid and virtual offices there are all kinds of things which can distract us during the day. Depending on where you are, at work or home, it could be an email or text that popped up. It might be a meeting. It could be laundry or the dishes from last night. While all those things are important, there's usually one enormous project which requires your undivided attention and if you gave it your full attention, you'd probably be finished with it in half the time it's taking, if you didn't allow yourself to become distracted.

Ever reach the end of the day and don't feel as though you have accomplished a thing, or at least not the "thing" that you most wanted to finish? You were working on one project only to get distracted or sidetracked by the next shiny object or what you think needs your attention right now? Then, at the end of the day, it doesn't feel like you finished anything— because you didn't!

It's like the little mouse in the book *If You Give a Mouse a Cookie*. You're cleaning your house or garage, and one project leads to another. You'll start putting away the dishes. The cupboard is overflowing, so you begin organizing it. Something spills on the floor, and not only do you clean it up, but you decide it's time to mop the floor. You get the mop and notice the laundry room needs organizing. When organizing, you realize you need laundry detergent and begin your grocery list. You get the picture.

While writing this book, Ann started to write and then got distracted by the next shiny object. She jumped from one idea to the next. Maybe she should work on her blog article, podcast, or website or blah, blah, blah. At the end of the day, she still hadn't edited a single chapter, let alone finished one. She asked herself, "What did I do? I did many "things," and yet did I finish what I said was truly important to me? No. Did I allow myself to become distracted? Yes." She asked herself, "Why did I allow myself to get distracted?"

Finally, after taking several breaths and talking to a trusted friend, she settled on one way to share all the information bouncing around in her head.

Like you, Ann has many ideas about what she still wants to do in life, such as where she wants to take her business, and books she wants to write. She sometimes allows herself to become mentally paralyzed. No judgment, just choices to make. She, like you, gets to decide what idea or path to pursue. It's a lifelong challenge, figuring out how to navigate all the choices and paths to pursue.

I get blamed for distracting the team by giving them lots of ideas, projects, and tasks to do. What I'm providing you and your team with are different paths to take. The trick is for you to determine which path to take at what time and to stick to it.

What do you do when you see the next shiny object and feel you just have to go after it? Why is it so easy to become distracted? What distracts you at work and home? At work or school, maybe it's FOMO—you know, the fear of missing out. Are you afraid of missing out if you don't pursue the next best idea? But what if it isn't? If you jump from one thing to another with me and without completing the first, it's hard to feel a sense of accomplishment because nothing really gets finished or doesn't get finished in the time you'd like it to.

One of Ann's favorite memories, permanently embedded in her mind, is of her son, Noah, when he was about four years old. They were at a park waiting for other kids and their moms to arrive. He spotted a squirrel that looked like a lot of fun to play with. He chased that squirrel, who zigzagged around the park until the squirrel scurried up a tree. Exhausted from chasing him, he made his way back to her for a quick rest and a cherry juice box until the next squirrel appeared and he was off. Ever feel as if you're zigzagging all over the place chasing ideas? I do, but then again, I'm the squirrel!

So why do we get distracted?

Ann and her friends shared some reasons they become distracted down below! Check them out, OK? They also shared ideas about how they refocus in the strategy section.

Reasons we get distracted and what distracts us.

- Stress or worry about all the details, and not wanting to miss anything, boredom, or frustrations with the current task (Janet).
- My long list of to-dos distracts me!! (Lisa S.).
- Texts and emails.
- Too many commitments.
- Acting on an idea at the moment in which you have the idea.
- Not being fully present in the moment.
- Details may be boring and tedious.
- Bored with the original activity and what I'm doing at the time (Lisa S.).
- Overwhelmed with a project, for example, doing laundry and seeing *my closet needs straightening* (Alison).
- The new project looks more fun than what I'm currently working on.
- Just not that interested in the original project.
- It's taking too long to finish the project or see progress being made.
- FOMO (fear of missing out).

The distractions you allow to impede doing what you want or need to focus on are different from things that come up that need to be done or that are interruptions you may not be able to control. For example, your supervisor may call a meeting or need something right away. True, this is an interruption and maybe it is a distraction. However, it's one of those things that needs to be done and is important. A customer may ask a question. Sometimes, distractions or "interruptions" are part of the job.

The good news—you get to decide what is important at the time. If you have a team member that listens to me, their personal squirrel, you can help them with figuring out how to finish an activity and not just run amuck.

What can we do to lead our squirrel brain? Not shut it down, lead it. I challenge you to embrace me and let me serve you. Work with me and do *not* let me take over.

The challenge doesn't lie in the choices you have,
it's the challenge in determining which of the choices
are the priority at any given moment in time.

Piles and Piles of Projects: Distractions? Or not?

Ann's husband exhibits a great deal of organization, analytical thinking, and focus. He likes things to have a place and keeps them in it. While all of us possess a variety of characteristics and are a mixture of the styles ourselves, everyone has their natural behavior and own way of doing things. While Ann likes organization, she usually has a million projects going on at the same time. She works on keeping her office and life organized, but the truth is she lives life using the pile method. She has piles of projects. It's getting better as she has acquired a huge file cabinet, and folder holders for the many manila file folders that litter her life.

Instead of making herself crazy worrying about what others think and changing who she is, Ann has taken on a different mindset. Instead of being obsessed with all the piles in her office, her new mindset is this: she is lucky to have many awesome projects going on. Your very active team member, with the squirrel brain, has many interests and approaches, all of them with a wealth of enthusiasm. I, the squirrel, am quick and playful, chattering constantly, sharing ideas, and creating chaos in your mind. Doug is a master at leading his squirrel brain. Ann still has a ways to go.

Cindy Becomes a Master Gardener—Leading her Squirrel in the Direction Right for Her

Cindy had a dream. She dreamed of becoming a master gardener. For years, she put it off and allowed "things" to get in her way. Like many people who put off doing things they want to do because they think and sometimes are busy with jobs, taking care of things like paying the bills, and taking care of others, which, by the way, are all important. It is also important to remember your dreams and goals. Ann and Cindy worked together. The positive energy radiated from Cindy as she talked about her dream.

Ann asked her how important it was to become a master Gardener and what it would take for her to realize her dream. Cindy said that she needed to attend and complete a certification program to become a master gardener. This was no small feat during a pandemic. It would take applying for the class, time to complete the class (possibly virtually), determination, and dedication to outside class work to achieve the goal. She determined her goal was in fact important and was tired of just thinking about it. She made time to write down the action steps needed to achieve her goal. She then implemented and followed through with her plan which is key. Cindy sent Ann an email in the Spring of 2022 and shared she was graduating as a master gardener. Excitement and pride shone through her email. I'm uncertain who was more excited—Cindy or Ann. Okay, Ann was probably second, but I can assure you, she was a close second!

Alison Cleans Up Dog Poop and Stops to Make a Phone Call

Ann's friend, Alison, is one of the Queen Squirrel Brains. She has millions of things going on in her mind and thinks of things at the most interesting moments. Ann is a Norwex consultant. Norwex is about cleaning without chemicals. Alison is one of the few people who can call Ann and tell her she thought of her when she was cleaning up the dog's accident, aka, poop, in the house. Why is Ann not offended? Because Alison uses Norwex and knows Norwex cloths will clean up the mess and remove the bacteria in her house, hence making it greener and cleaner for Alison and her family.

While others may just shake their heads, they laugh and continue to share moments like this. You can't make this stuff up, and girls really do just want to have fun.

Ann and the Fabric Store—Customers and Interruptions or Responsibility?

When I was talking to Ann, she shared this story... Years ago, when she managed a fabric store, there was a time that she worked on a major fabric order and kept getting "interrupted" by customers or team members who needed help. Her thought process went like this, "I'm never going to get this order finished if I keep getting interrupted."

That statement was accurate. However, the "interruptions," her customers and supporting her team members, were the most important part of her job at that moment. They were her entire job! What did she do to finish fabric orders in a timelier manner, which she had to do every other week? She changed her schedule.

On the days orders were placed, Ann would come in an hour or two before the store opened and complete the order, without interruption or distractions, in easily a fourth of the time it would have taken here if the store was open. Now I get it—not everyone can come in an hour early, but maybe you can negotiate uninterrupted quiet time to work on a project. Though you also have to be willing to stop interrupting yourself, which can be the biggest challenge of all.

Lessons Learned

- You have a wealth of ideas and opportunities—embrace and manage them.

- You have what it takes and the resources you need to be successful.

- It's okay to ask for help.

- Everyone has moments or days when it's a challenge to focus on those challenging projects, answer all those emails, texts, and phone calls. It can be a challenge to address the ones that aren't taxing on the brain like the dishes or laundry.

- Once you focus and finish one project, you can move onto the next "shiny" object of choice.

- You can have multiple projects going on, you just have to manage them and decide which one is the most important to work on first. The potential result of not making or delaying a decision because of not knowing which direction to take may be made for you through procrastination.

- Figure out what you do and don't want in life. Knowing what you do *not* want is of equal importance to knowing what you *do* want. Focus on what you want.

- Embrace your squirrel and let him have his freedom. He will serve you well. Just remember to let your other team members work side by side with, not in *competition with*, your squirrel.

- Remove the distractions of everyday life. Do you need a change of venue? With so many people working at home, sometimes the lines are blurred between your personal and professional life. Occasionally, the library or a coffee shop can be a great place to work—you're away from your normal environment and some distractions at home or the office. Ann's friend Stan suggested she go to a coffee shop when she shared with him, she was stuck on her first draft. All she could do was look around and see the things that needed to be done. It was easy to interrupt herself with everything other than working on this book. She took his advice—and it worked great. The background "noise," the chatter of friends solving the problems of the world in the coffee shop and music in her ear didn't distract. Like Goldilocks in the home of the three bears, the coffee shop was—not too quiet, not too loud, but just right.

"You can have it all. Just not all at once."

Oprah Winfrey

My Strengths

- I give you lots of ideas and choices.

- I challenge you to think about what's important now.

Your Strengths (List the strengths you see in yourself when it comes to realizing how distractions and interruptions are showing up and a willingness to choose my priorities.)

Strategies: Choose the one(s) which will best serve you.

- Remember your "WHY" and what's important to you. Write it down. Put it where you can easily see or refer to it.

- Make a list of your ideas. Put them in a notebook, a document on your computer or on a thumb drive or in the note section of your phone. This way you keep them in a safe space, yet don't have to worry about remembering all of them. Nine times out of ten, you will forget the idea if you don't write it down right away. If you are driving, please don't text and drive. Pull over and write it down. Writing things down helps you remember your "to-do" or "will-do" list.

- Set aside time to make your list, though it's the "in-the-moment distractions that can be the challenge."

- Take a deep breath, think, and repeat—one thought at a time. One task at a time. One day at a time (Deanna).

- Write about your hopes, dreams, and projects you want to do and have to do. Don't worry or be concerned right now about the how—that comes later. If you want to make a bucket list, do it. List anywhere from one to 99 things. Challenge yourself to choose a certain number. For example, five of the most important things then make a realistic timetable of when you want to accomplish them. You can always adjust the timetable.

- Lift it up in prayer and ask for God's help in refocusing (Janet).

- A coach once shared with me "How to WIN" Remember "What's Important Now." This helps to stay focused on what you're doing right now and being more present (Lisa S.).

- Stop and remember the task at hand. Focus on it—not the surrounding things. Take a quick time-out and focus on what you really want or need to accomplish (Alison).

- Negotiate with your team for uninterrupted time for you or maybe for your entire team when no one schedules meetings or "drops" in (unless, of course, it's an emergency) to chat or to ask questions. This gives everyone time to focus on those big projects at hand.

- List the activities on paper. It's easier to see, organize, and prioritize them, then decide which project is the most important to work on first.

  - Ann loves a good list. What she really likes is to check things off when she completes the task. If she does something and it's not on the list, she adds it to the list just so she can check it off—how funny is that? Oh, so some of you are laughing your heads off, because either you are thinking seriously, *why would anyone do that,* and the rest of you are thinking, *that is so me.* Embrace who you are.

- Make a Ninety-Nine-Item Bucket list. List 99 things you want to accomplish or do. The first ten will be easy, the next eighty-nine won't be. I encourage you to dig deep and make that list. If you have a partner, have your partner create his/her list. Are there any things you might like to do together? It's a great way for partners and/or families to plan projects, trips, and experiences to do together.

- Create a parking lot—in other words, make a place to store your ideas so you have them when you need them but don't have to remember them in your mind. She is working to combine her parking lots. Currently, Ann's parking lot is on her phone, her little black book with mind maps of ideas, files on the computer, and, of course, post-it notes (because she is the queen of post-it notes). There is currently a sea of post-it notes (around one hundred) stuck to the upper half of her desk. Normally, this might make her crazy. However, when her husband asked her what they were, she told him they were her brain and books on post-it notes. They inspire her to keep going. He just shook his head and laughed.

- Time Blocking

  ◦ Ann works well and is most productive when she has a block of time to focus on a project. Now I get it. Sometimes the only block of time you seem to have is 15 minutes. But is it? If it is, ask yourself what can you get done in 15 minutes? Maybe it's checking email or writing a quick memo. At home, maybe it's doing the dishes or folding the laundry. However, if you have a major project, how can you schedule time blocks and when?

- Put deadlines and dates for action steps on the calendar.

- Get an accountability partner (someone who will support you in a positive manner) and share your plan with them.

- Block a meeting on your calendar—with yourself—to begin, work on, or finish that big project.

- Determine your priorities.

- Make a plan and stick to it.

- Make a Will-Do list with a timeline.

- Turn off your email and silence your phone for a short time if possible.

- Make a conscious effort to remain focused on the task at hand.

- Work on the project when you're at your best or when you do your best work. This is the time to schedule your most challenging projects. For example, if writing up a proposal takes a lot of your energy and if you're a morning person, work on it in the morning. If you're more productive in the afternoon, work on it in the afternoon.

- Pivot with a purpose— Alter the course if it gets you back on track or if there is a better path to take to get to the destination.

- Stop—just because it made sense at one time or another or when we started, based on a change in priorities, resources, or something along the way, maybe the team or I need to stop working toward the goal.

- List your ideas and all things that have distracted you in the past or might in the future. Acknowledge them. Decide how to eliminate or reduce them. This way, you will have them in one place where you can review them.

"We cannot direct the wind, but we can adjust the sails."

Dolly Parton

Your Reflection

Reflection Questions: Answer here or in a separate journal.

1. Where do I want/need to pause, ponder, pivot, and proceed?

2. Where can I think and work without distractions?

3. What are the things which distract me the most?

4. What are the actual reasons I allow myself to be distracted?

5. What am I willing to do to remain focused?

Your Biggest Take-away(s) Regarding Distractions and Interruptions

Your Action Plan

Here is an example of what your action plan may look like. Remember it's your plan not mine, this is only an example to support you in getting started. Choose the action that will support you in moving forward. There is space for you to write your personal plan of action at the end of the example.

1. *Goal: Reduce interruptions*

2. *Action: Make a list of things which interrupt my work and determine how to reduce each interruption. With regard to email, I will turn off notifications. While working on a major project I will share with people that I need an hour of uninterrupted time unless there's an emergency. I will set a timer for 60 minutes and not look at social media during that time.*

3. *Who will support me? Peer(s) at work. Family when I'm at home.*

4. *Date: September 3rd.*

5. *How will I know I'm making progress? I will have notifications turned off and schedule uninterrupted time on the calendar each day.*

Your Turn: Answer here or in a separate journal.

1. Goal:
2. Action:
3. Who can support you?
4. Date to begin:
5. How will you know you made progress?

As you can see, I love running here and there checking out all of the choices life has to offer. Next, you'll meet my good buddy the tortoise. He takes things a good deal slower than I do. However, there are advantages to this approach too. Like the rest of us, your tortoise brings value to the team.

Additional Resources

- *12 Week Year* by Brian P. Moran, Michael Lennington.
- *Ignite* by Mitch Matthews.

The Tortoise

Patience and Perseverance

"Remember, slow and steady wins the race."

Leyasu Tokugawa

Most of you are familiar with the story of the Tortoise and the Hare. You know, the one where the hare looked at me, the tortoise, laughed, and figured he would have an easy time winning the race. The hare thought that because it took me so long to go a few feet, he had plenty of time to get to the end of the route and win the race. He took a nap and didn't realize how much patience and perseverance I had when I set my mind to something. In the end, I won the race!

However, it's not about beating anyone, it was about me putting my nose to the grindstone, and having the patience and perseverance to keep going, to get where I wanted to go. It is important to pay attention to what your competition is doing and of equal importance to pay attention to what you're doing to achieve the result you want.

Do your goals excite you? You know that feeling where you can hardly wait to get started and achieve them, only to feel as if it is taking *forever* to reach your goal, finish that project, or for the start of your vacation to get here? I know just how you feel. Ann knows how you feel. She didn't think she would *ever* get this book written. Tired of hearing about this? So was she.

Time is a well-sought-after commodity. To find or make enough time and have the patience to work on your goal or project is sometimes a challenge, especially when it seems as if it's taking a long time to see and feel progress. How do you feel when it seems as if it's taking you or a team member a long time to finish a project?

How many of you like to see the fruits of your labor quickly? I'm good at taking my time to work for something, though it's hard for my friends to wait for results. Ann likes to see them, if not immediately, at best, sooner rather than later.

The geese help me remember that you don't have to be the fastest, but you do have to keep moving forward toward your goal, even if it's taking more time than you'd like. So why does it take me so much time to get where I want to go and how do I remember to have patience or persevere?

Have you ever stayed focused, even when progress seemed slow?

Ann is the type of person who likes to see results in a short time. She discovered she likes to sew because she can sew one or two seams together and see progress in a heartbeat. She likes to crochet but does not like to knit because it takes so darn long to make any significant progress you can see. Knit one. Purl two. Good grief, this is taking all day! She wants to note, however, that her grandmother, who she admired and learned to sew from, used to knit and even had her own yarn shop. Ann just didn't get the knitting gene and that's OK. You are an individual, not the people around you. In other words, you're a part of the team, and it's important all these parts are different! She still has a sweater her grandmother made and treasures it. It is beautiful and full of intricate detail.

She knows what her dad taught her is true—"Anything worth having is worth working for." It's kind of like overnight success takes about ten years. She just didn't know that sometimes the work behind the scenes, while not "sexy," is important. It's like the foundation of a house. Perhaps one of the most boring parts of the house, but argumentatively, it is perhaps the most important.

Ann's husband and son are very analytical and methodical. They think before they speak and always have something thoughtful and meaningful to say. She could learn to do this more often. It's just hard for her to wait until they're ready to talk. I am sure it's equally hard for them when she is talking a hundred miles an hour and firing questions at them before they've even processed the first question and digested all her ramblings. Can you relate to either or both styles? See yourself or others in the above scenario?

Sometimes Ann feels like me, in the story of the Tortoise and the Hare. She feels as if it's taking forever to get where she wants to be. While you're not in a race with anyone, it may feel like it. A slower pace, while sometimes the pace she needs, is so hard for Ann. Is it for you? Ever feel like you're in a race with yourself?

Success means different things to different people. I think that's where the Big P's come in—patience and perseverance. If you can figure out why what you're doing is important and what's important to the team, your supervisor, or the company, it can be easier, not easy—but easier to keep going until you're finished. In a world filled with email, texting, and social media, where instant gratification seems like the norm, my values can get lost and forgotten. It's important to remember that life is not about the biggest house, who has the most money, or what is perceived as the most important title at work. Let's face it—everyone is important just in different ways. Patience and perseverance are a challenge to teach and even more challenging to experience, even though this is how most of us learn them. Short-term pain. Long-term gain.

People sometimes interchangeably use perseverance and persistence. They can have a similar meaning but are very different. Perseverance is when you keep moving toward your goal even when obstacles get in your way, and you weather the storm knowing you are on the right path. Persistence is when you stay the course no matter what, even when the best choice might be to change the course.

Patience and perseverance can stand alone or work together because sometimes when you need to persevere, you need patience. And sometimes, perseverance means that you have the patience to see something through to the end.

Taking more time than what you or others think it "should" take to finish might sometimes be mistaken for laziness or lack of motivation. Motivation plays a role in getting things done, however so do patience and perseverance. In the race with the hare, my motivation was to just finish, and I relied on patience and perseverance the entire time.

Patience

Doug, Ann's husband, is a very patient man. He possesses the admirable quality of taking time to think and taking great care with how he answers a question. He thinks before he speaks. If he isn't sure of an answer or doesn't know, he will research or Google something on his phone. He takes forever, or so it seems to Ann, for him to share his thoughts.

She is quick to answer questions, which sometimes serves her well and other times, not so much.

Ever think, "Oh. My. Gosh. Will the person ever finish or get their thoughts and ideas out?"

However, when the person does say something, people listen because they have taken the time to really think about things before speaking. Ann values and admires the time and effort people put into their thoughts. She reminds herself of the importance of this gift I bring to the team and how it serves all involved.

With patience, I give my team members time to think. I give you time to think and work through the situation. When Ann went through her coaching certification, she learned a valuable acronym that she remembers and asks herself still today in many situations, especially when she finds herself talking and losing patience when "waiting" for someone. It continues to serve her well to this day.

The acronym is "W.A.I.T." It stands for "Why Am I Talking?"

She also added an 's' to it. "W.A.I.S.T." "Why Am I Still Talking?"

She can at least laugh at herself. That's important!

Perseverance

What happens when obstacles get in your way?

Sometimes, when I sense there are obstacles ahead, I clam up and stick my head inside my shell to stay safe. The eagle then gives me confidence to stick my neck out to see what possibilities lie ahead.

In my case, some obstacles that I face include my short legs, the speed at which I travel, and maybe even letting others' perceptions of me cloud my vision. However, persevering is about staying the course or adjusting it if need be, as well as figuring out how to overcome the obstacles in your way. My short legs weren't changing, but I found a way to use what I had, and I kept walking without taking long breaks like my friend the hare.

I stayed the course. Allowing what others think of you can be an obstacle that's hard to tackle—so enlist help. In my case, I knew what success meant and that day it was merely finishing the race. However, it's not always that easy.

What do you do when obstacles get in your way? What are some obstacles you are working to overcome? Some may lie with my friends, like finding your self-confidence, making decisions, and beating procrastination. Let your team members and the strategies in this book support you in overcoming the obstacles you face. The worst thing you can do is ignore them.

For Ann, perseverance is when you keep moving forward on something, even when it's hard or in the midst of obstacles seen or unforeseen. For example, you may be writing a book, working on a certification, returning to school as a non-traditional student, or leading a meeting or project for the first time. You keep moving forward to achieve your goal or whatever it is you are working on, overcoming obstacles until you accomplish your goal.

> *"Obstacles are those frightful things you see when you take your eyes off your goals."*
>
> *Henry Ford*

Lynn, Her Business and COVID

Lynn and Ann met at Mitch's Mastermind and attended a weekend workshop together. While there, people asked Lynn what she did. She shared that she and her husband, Nick, owned The Hall, in West Des Moines.

Ann said, "Oh, the one at 111 South 11th Street in West Des Moines?"

With an astonished look on her face, Lynn said that most people hadn't even heard of it yet, let alone know the exact address, as it was a fairly new business. Ann laughed and revealed that she had just been to an event at The Hall a couple of weeks before, and had no idea why the address was ingrained in her brain. Maybe it was all the ones! It really is a small world—you never know who you are going to meet and when.

Like with many, COVID threw a monkey wrench into Lynn's hopes, dreams, plans, and even her business. Lynn had multiple conversations with her husband about how they would make it through, coming out successfully at the other end of COVID-19, though neither really knew the answers to how they were going to make it. How would they manage the uncertainty surrounding their two new businesses: The Hall, an amazing place for groups from two to two hundred to gather (yet no one could gather during COVID), and The Justice League, a nonprofit focused on reducing hunger and homelessness in Central Iowa by teaching young people from low economic income areas culinary skills?

Meeting the obstacles COVID so viciously put in front of them was no match for Lynn and Nick. They knew the importance of their businesses to others and figured out how to answer each obstacle placed in front of them. It wasn't going to be easy, but it was doable, together.

Lynn experienced an unexpected gift from COVID. The beauty of time. Time spent in the quiet of her own mind thinking about what really mattered. They knew they could lose it all: the businesses, their home, their peace of mind. Lynn and Nick knew a business, a house, and material things did not define who they were.

"Stuff wasn't us," said Lynn, during one conversation with Ann.

While there are certain things they could not control, there were others they could—their mindset, their actions, and how they used the finite resources they had. They asked themselves what they could do not only to stay afloat, but of equal importance—how could they help those who didn't have resources and were not as fortunate as they were? They thought about all the people who were going to need help and who were not used to asking for it, letting alone accepting it. It would take seven—eight weeks into the pandemic for people to begin receiving benefits. That's a long time without a normal income to purchase even the bare necessities such as food.

Lynn and Nick launched an online Pop-up Pantry with restaurant-quality food for just over wholesale cost. They teamed up with The Distillery, which occupied space right next to The Hall, to distribute sandwiches and sanitizer twice a week. This conversation happened on a Thursday and two days later, on Saturday, they were up and running sandwiches and sanitizer.

By helping others, they continued to remember how extremely fortunate they were. Today, The Hall and The

Justice League are thriving. People gather at The Hall for business and pleasure, but most importantly, for conversations which continue to build and strengthen relationships. The Justice League's tradition of teaching culinary skills to aspiring chefs and bakers lives on. In the end, perseverance and patience worked!

Noah, the Black Belt, and the Paper

Even at a young age, Noah, Ann's son, has learned a great deal about perseverance. When the going gets tough, the tough keep going.

Noah is a black belt in American Kempo Karate. He studied karate for nearly ten years, from ages six to 16. While he earned his first-grade black belt in sixth grade, his goal was to earn his first-degree black belt and break a brick. Once you earn your first black belt, you can only test every six months, so it took several years to earn the five grades of black belt needed to be eligible to test for the first-degree black belt. One of his goals was to test with his dad as they were both working toward his black belt.

The one time that Doug tested for his black belt, Noah had a rough day and didn't qualify to test when Doug did. It would have been easy to quit because he was already a black belt, involved in school, sports, and Scouts working toward the Eagle Scout. However, after several conversations, and remembering the long-term goal of breaking a brick, he decided to stick with karate and continue training and testing. Ann is proud to share that Noah broke that brick in the spring of his sophomore year and earned his first-degree black belt.

In his junior year at the University of Iowa, Noah decided to do an honors project, which was not a requirement to graduate. It consisted of writing and presenting a research paper. As a prerequisite to writing the paper he had to complete a class which prepared students for the project. He completed the class. The next step—research and write the paper during his senior year. He talked with one of his professors about his idea and asked her to serve as his advisor, to which she said yes.

Noah's paper: *Crime and Compensation: An Analysis of Wages, Unemployment, and Government Assistance,* focused on income and its effect on crime rates. This was a timely and relevant topic.

Writing is not his first, second, or even third love. He can write but doesn't enjoy it. In January 2022, he had a choice—finish the project after putting it off for a long time or withdraw from the class.

Ann and Doug shared that they supported Noah, no matter what he decided. It was his decision. They would not tell him what to do. With decisions, we all have to live with the consequences, no matter if they are positive or negative. As much as Noah would have liked to have withdrawn from the class, he didn't want to quit. He decided to finish the paper and the class. You see, growing up the policy in his family was that you always finish what you started.

The weekend prior to the research fair, he went home to have quiet time to finish the research for his paper and create his poster for the research fair. On Saturday night, when Ann and Doug left to play cards, Noah was diligently working on the information for his poster. Returning home around midnight, Ann and Doug found their son at the center island in the kitchen reviewing the data and just shaking his head.

Upon examining the results of his calculations, Noah recognized that the coefficients of some variables seemed incorrect or in his words "way off". He knew if something seemed wrong, he needed to double-check his process to ensure his conclusions were not a result of an incorrect course of action.

Based on the published crime rates of the two columns impacted it was clear that the numbers were simply flipped by the original author of the information. Upon this discovery he inserted the data into the intended fields, correcting the mistake resulting in an analysis that while still giving surprising results, was a more realistic analysis of the information.

The three of them examined the data and assessed the recording of the other rows and columns was correct. It was only those two columns that appeared to be wrong. Noah noted his findings in the research paper since sources are cited. At three in the morning, Noah recalculated the results and was ready to send the information for the poster to Staples. Doug picked up the poster early Sunday afternoon as Noah continued working on the paper. The poster looked great. Noah presented at the research fair. He finished the paper and earned an "A" in the class.

While Ann and Doug were excited about his grade, they told him what they were most proud of was the fact he stuck to it even after multiple obstacles got in his way and would have made it easy to say, "I'm not finishing this because I'm exhausted."

The perseverance learned through past experiences supported him in keeping his eye on his desire to finish what he started and complete the paper and the honors class.

"Anything in Life Worth Having is Worth Working For"

Andrew Carnegie

Ann Keeps Plugging Away on the Book

When Ann decided she really wanted to write a book, it felt as if she would never finish. Patience doesn't come easy to Ann. She prays for patience, and she'd like that patience to arrive right now. She knows anything worth having is worth waiting and working for. Yet, many times like when writing this book, she wants things done and to be able to see results sooner rather than later. She could work for hours, and it was hard to "see" the progress because it was on the computer. When she started, it was a slow process just figuring out which book she wanted to write first and getting her head wrapped around the entire process and then breaking it down into manageable steps.

It took what seemed like forever to get here. Publishing her first book! What made her persevere? She had always wanted to write a book, so this was a personal commitment to herself. Her determination in wanting to set a good example for Noah that when you set a goal and really want to do something, keep your eye on the end result and work hard to achieve it, played a key role in finding the desire to keep going. The support and faith of her family and friends in her helped her persevere. It took a village and many of the "friends" you've met in this book to get her to the end of this book, so she and Noah can begin on the next one.

Too many people stop or close the door just before they are about to make it through the change or reach their goal. Remember how the butterfly perseveres? What if it stopped just before it broke through that last layer of the cocoon? What if it had stopped just before the life, it had been working so hard to achieve revealed itself? Are you stopping just before you turn the corner of where your dreams and goals are waiting for you? Sometimes, when things are hard or unclear, it's easy to wonder if you're on the right path. If you kept your eyes on the dream, knowing the "obstacles" that get in your way are temporary and there to make you stronger and help you reach your destination, would you keep going?

Lessons Learned

- We all bring value to the relationship—just at a different pace, even from those who take a little longer to think things through.
- You are the only one who can determine if you want to persevere.
- Patience is a virtue. If it's worth having. It's worth working and waiting for.
- Slow and steady wins the race.
- Appreciate the time and energy it takes to complete a quality project.
- You don't have to do it alone. Rely on your support system. And if you don't have a support system yet, that's OK. Find one at home, at work, in social organizations, volunteering, or at church. Keep looking, it's there. Have patience and persevere.

My Strengths

- I encourage you to work to finish what you started, no matter how long it takes.
- I inspire you to take the time required to do what you're working on well.
- I provide you with patience.
- I will help you overcome the obstacles placed before you.

Your Strengths (List the strengths you see in yourself when it comes to patience and perseverance.)

Strategies: Choose the one(s) which will best serve you.

- Focus on the outcome or goal(s).
- Make and take time to think and write about your priorities and ideas.
- Write down steps needed to complete your project and assign a timeline to each—this will help you persevere.
- Celebrate small wins.
- Remember your reason for doing the project (your future, it's part of your job, what you'll learn from it, etc.).
- Research, but don't let it paralyze your progress.
- Evaluate alternatives.
- Collaborate with friends, peers, and other organizations.
- Post your goal somewhere it can be seen and remind you of what you are working on.
- Put time in your calendar to think.
- Lynn takes a purposeful pause similar to Ann's pause with cause.
- Mitch Mathews shares in the Acceleration Mastermind and challenges us to remember:
  - Recognize what you can control.
  - Identify what you can influence.
  - Accept what you can't control and set it aside.
  - Patience comes to those who are open to it and make an effort to exercise it.

Your Reflection

Reflection Questions: Answer here or in a separate journal.

1. When was the last time I exemplified patience?

2. When did I choose to persevere even when it was difficult and how did it feel to stick to my goal?

3. What strategies have I used and what new ones do I want to try?

4. What strategies will help me remember to have patience and persevere, and what strategies will I use the next time patience and perseverance can and need to be my friends?

Your Biggest Take-away(s) Regarding Patience and Perseverance

Your Action Plan

Here is an example of what your action plan may look like. Remember it's your plan not mine, this is only an example to support you in getting started. Choose the action which will support you in moving forward. There is space for you to write your personal plan of action at the end of the example.

1. *Goal: Persevere until the second book is published.*

2. *Action: Focus on the outcome or goal Noah and I have for the second book and work to remember the reason we are doing it. I will write down the outcome and place it somewhere that I can see it every single day. We will determine a timeline for the book and talk with each other every other week to record the progress each of us is making.*

3. *Who will support me? My husband and Noah, as well as, my coach.*

4. *Date: November 1st.*

5. *How will I know I'm making progress? Noah and I will reach the benchmarks we set and publish the book by Spring of 2025.*

Your Turn: Answer here or in a separate journal.

1. Goal:

2. Action:

3. Who can support you?

4. Date to begin:

5. How will you know you made progress?

As we are nearing the end of our journey together there's one more team member we want you to meet. The final member of our team ties everything we continue to learn in life together. Let's see what the wise old owl has to say.

Additional Resources

- *The Power of Patience: How This Old-Fashioned Virtue Can Improve Your Life* by M.J. Ryan.
- *Grit* by Angela Duckworth.
- *The 12 Week Year* by Brian Moran.

The Owl
Wisdom

"Knowledge is knowing what to say.
Wisdom is knowing when to say it."

Unknown

*E*ver say something, then gasp, and think, "Oh no, did I just say that out loud?"

As the quote for this chapter states, knowledge is knowing what to say. Wisdom is knowing when to say something, and I may add, whether or not to say it all.

As the wise old owl, I am the final team member you'll meet on this particular journey. Why am I last? Because my friends, the geese, recognize I have the distinct honor of helping you realize how much knowledge and wisdom you've acquired over the years. I'm hoping by investing the time to read about my friends, we've helped you gain insight and appreciation for the gifts and strengths each of us brings even though at first it may be hard to see.

Do you ever think to yourself, *why couldn't I just be born with the knowledge and skills needed to succeed in life? Life would be so much easier!* Or would it? On the surface, it sounds great, yet in reality, would all that knowledge mean as much to you as it does when you have to learn it through experience? There's something to be said about what is gained through sweat equity and the trials and tribulations and obstacles you overcome in life to achieve your goals and get where you want to be.

Are there times you wish you could transfer what you learned to others to save them and you the time and sometimes heartache or grief of figuring it out on their own? The only problem with this is that it's like many multiple-choice exams. You memorize it for the test and forget it the next day. When you learn through your own unique experiences, you're more likely to internalize the lessons and really learn them. This way when you're in the same or similar position in the future, the knowledge and skills are part of who you are and easier to apply because you learned them, not just memorized them.

Knowledge and wisdom can look different for everyone.

This can also be challenging because sometimes people think they are wise just because they have a great deal of knowledge. However, like I shared earlier it's one thing to have the information; it's totally different knowing when to apply the knowledge gained.

What are some of the ways in which you gain knowledge?
- Reading books
- Attending classes
- Life experiences
- Having conversations with people

From where do you gain wisdom?
- Knowledge.
- Life's trials and errors.
- Being willing to learn from your mistakes.

Knowledge can exist without wisdom, but not the other way around. Knowledge is the information you've learned and a component of wisdom. Wisdom is the ability to apply knowledge and use it in a meaningful and profound way. Wisdom goes beyond learning and memorizing facts. It means you have taken time to reflect and make sense of what you learned and how to use your knowledge wisely!

You may ask, "What is challenging about wisdom?"

The answer? It takes time to acquire it. Those mistakes you and everyone make serve a purpose. Wisdom is gained from what you learn by making them.

For Ann, wisdom turned out to be much more challenging to obtain than knowledge. Learning came easy. Learning when and how to share certain life lessons presented a challenge at times. Like many people, in her younger days, Ann thought she knew more than she did. Through experiences she gained the wisdom of knowing how to apply the knowledge gained and knowing when to share it as well as when to give others the chance to gain their wisdom through their own experiences. While she has learned much, this is still hard for her. She is a work-in-progress, just like everyone else.

It's mind-boggling to think about all the information you've learned in school. However, do you know how to apply it? During her early teaching days, Ann thought she needed to "teach" her students most if not all the information contained in the textbook. Because if she didn't "teach" them "everything," she wouldn't be doing her job. She had knowledge of the subject, knew how to develop exams, and lead discussions as well as relate to students. After a couple years of teaching, she gained wisdom on how to actually "teach." She doesn't "teach" her students anymore. Ann helps them *learn* as much as they can through them doing most of the work. She provides information, support, discussions, and a plethora of different ways in which they can learn and begin to apply the knowledge gained. This lesson was learned from someone at a conference who posed this question to a room full of educators, "Who is doing most of the work in class? You or your students?" It's not always beneficial to do things for people. What is beneficial is to *be there* for people.

Years ago, during a counseling session when she was going through her divorce, her counselor stated she seemed to have a lot of wisdom by what she shared. I think at the time, one of the things she shared was that the only person responsible for your happiness is yourself. Many people add happiness to your life but it's really up to you whether or not you choose to be happy. Asking or expecting someone else to "make" you happy is too much responsibility to place on any one person.

She laughed and said that she'd paid for that wisdom through the many circumstances she had the "opportunity" to experience through the divorce.

Like most parents, Ann had many things she wanted to teach Noah and have him experience in life. Parents want to see their kids happy, successful, and productive. They don't want to see them struggle, hurt, or sad. No matter how good anyone's childhood is, most want their child's experience to be even better.

People learn the most from their mistakes, if they let themselves. It's easy to think you're helping people by "saving" them from making mistakes and telling them how to do everything and making it easy on them. Ann once saw a sign in a room at Westwood elementary, where

Noah attended school, which said, "If you want to make it hard on your kids, make it easy on them." This is so true. Knowing that parents need to let their kids work for things and make mistakes is one thing. Wisdom comes in letting them learn from their mistakes and solving challenges on their own. It doesn't mean you don't give them a foundation and guidance; it just means you don't interfere with every conversation they have with a friend.

When the first girl Noah dated broke up with him, he experienced the normal sadness and rejection. Ann shared with him his feelings were his feelings and were natural, and that things would all work out. He would meet someone else and date again. Ann wanted to take away the pain but as you all know, that's not possible. She knew, as most people know, the majority of people, though there are a few exceptions, who date each other in high school don't end up being soul mates and getting married. Yet, that doesn't matter to a kid going through a plethora of emotions.

The wisdom came in being careful not to downplay the range of emotions he experienced in the moment.

She was there to listen, if he wanted to talk.

His wisdom gained: he shared he didn't need a girlfriend to be happy. Fast forward to his senior year. He dated the nicest young lady for the entire year. They had fun and had each other's backs. While they chose to go their separate ways after graduation, he looks back at that year and those experiences with great joy and gratitude for the year they had together.

Allowing a child to learn and gain knowledge from their experience prepares them for greater challenges that lie ahead in life. Learning to manage sadness would serve him well into the future when he experienced the loss of three family members and a close friend.

The bottom line—you will continue to gain wisdom if you remember to learn from all your experiences and learn how and when to apply it. You don't realize the depth of wisdom gained until days, weeks, months, or even years after learning the initial knowledge.

The good news—wisdom continues to be acquired throughout your lifetime.

> *"If you're the smartest person in the room,*
> *you're in the wrong room."*
>
> *Confucius*

Ann's Divorce & Friendships

Shelley and Cindy, two of Ann's friends, helped her learn valuable lessons during her divorce. While she gained a great deal of knowledge and wisdom through the divorce, here are two lessons learned that she would like me to share.

Ann had a really hard time with a divorce she didn't want. Having the ability to feel empathy for others when going through the divorce was hard! What Shelley, in a kind and caring way, helped her realize is this: depending on the experiences, knowledge, and wisdom you have gained, what to one person was not a big deal could be a huge deal to someone else!

For example, for a teenager, the breakup with a significant other, no matter the length of the courtship, is, for that person, the hardest thing they have had to experience. You may know, through your own experience and the wisdom you've acquired, there will be someone else better suited for them. They don't know it because this is their first time through it. In their world, it's as devastating as the divorce was in Ann's. To this day, thirty years later, that wisdom stays with Ann.

Ann has a hard time asking for help. One night when preparing to leave Cindy's house, she shared that she felt terrible "dumping" all her thoughts and problems on her friends. She didn't really feel as if she had much to offer any of them in return, as she was already stretched so thin. Cindy asked Ann how she felt when her friends leaned on her when times were tough. Ann answered she felt needed, great, and grateful that they trusted her and felt comfortable sharing things with her. She was happy to be there for her friends. Cindy felt the same way and shared, "Then let us be here for you and give us the same opportunity we give to you." Point taken. Lesson learned. Experience and knowledge shared by Cindy helped Ann gain wisdom about the give and take of friendship. It's not always about being the strong one. It's about being vulnerable and letting others be there to lean on when you need them.

Noah and Ann's Heated Conversation

Ann and Noah have a great relationship. They can have deep conversations about a variety of topics. She works hard to ask questions and let Noah figure things out on his own. Ann, like many parents, would give anything to "save" Noah from the heartache of learning things the hard way, especially when she can see what "needs" to be done and how to do it through her own years of making mistakes and gaining wisdom.

One night, however, while discussing interviews they had a major disagreement on how to follow up after an interview. Should a thank-you card be sent or is an email thanking the person conducting the interview sufficient? Ann rarely plays the I-have-more-experience card, but in this case, she shared with Noah based on years of experience, she knew the right thing to do or so she thought.

He disagreed.

She stated, "I know you may think I'm full of it, but in this case, I'm right."

Noah simply replied, "No, Mom, if you think that—you're wrong. I think you're right most of the time. In this case, I think I'm right and if I'm wrong, maybe I will just have to learn it the hard way, on my own."

They agreed to disagree. The conversation ended on a positive note. Ann learned Noah had more wisdom than she realized. Everyone brings value to the team, even at the most unexpected times. The lessons parents can learn from their kids if they would just listen.

How did things turn out? Noah decided to send an email to thank the person who interviewed him for this particular interview. While he didn't get this job, he did receive a job offer from a different company, where he sent a "thank you" via email. For certain things, such as gifts received in the mail, he has chosen to send a handwritten thank you note or call or text the person who sent the gift.

In the end, perhaps what matters the most is the fact that Noah understands the importance of thanking someone and sending thanks to them in some way.

Dr. Lindeman: Knowledge and Wisdom Learned from Someone Who's Been There

Dr. Jen Lindeman, the principal at the time Ann's son was in high school, gave brilliant advice to the parents at the senior parent meeting at the beginning of the year. She shared that the year would be filled with many emotions, memories, and moments. Minds and hearts would overflow with the emotions of so many "lasts." Hope and anxiety about what the future would hold for each of their kiddos would creep into the equation. Memories of when they were little would forever be held in their hearts and fill their minds. While the past and future are important in looking at and planning, she encouraged them to remember to be present and enjoy the moments of their senior's final year of high school. The year would quickly come and go. Ann took her advice and enjoyed every single moment.

She and I encourage you to do the same. Whether it's a child's senior year, or life in general, enjoy the moments and make memories, for they will guide you in the decisions you make for your future.

The Little Team Learns a Lifelong Lesson

When Ann's son was about ten, he was a member of the Ankeny Junior Football organization, a team consisting of many average players. He was one of their average players. He worked hard, but he was there for the friends, the snacks, and oh, maybe to play some football. They named their team "Smashers." How does she remember this? She still has the little trophy she received when she was Team Mom for his team. She remembers this season like it was yesterday. They won five out of six games. She believes to this day, the key to their success was the fact that the coaches saw greatness in each person and helped them develop their individual strengths, as well as supporting them in learning how to work together to succeed.

They were on their way to a perfect season when, in the excitement of the moment, a coach's decision changed the outcome of the last game. In the final minutes of game number six, one of the coaches, instead of just letting the time run out and kneeling the ball, had the quarterback pass the ball to one of the running backs. Instead of running the ball in for an unneeded touchdown, he fumbled it, and the other team recovered and ran it in for a touchdown. The coach, the boy who dropped the ball, and the team were deflated and devastated.

The good news—the moment passed quickly. The boys didn't blame the kid who fumbled, the coach didn't yell, and they learned no one is perfect, no team is perfect, no decision is perfect. In losing the game, they learned how to act with dignity, how to console and support their team member who was feeling pretty low, and how to lose with grace, which in reality is winning.

It's not always about the number on a scoreboard which can quickly change in a game, it was about the team and what each player brought to the table. It's not that one player was so much better or that there were only one or two superstars on the team. It was allowing each boy to capitalize on his strength. They were stronger together, because of each other, not because of only one player. Just like you are stronger because of your team within and your team members on the outside.

The season may have been over, yet the lesson continues to this day—how to win and lose with grace, dignity, and integrity.

Noah and the Paper — The Animals Work Together. Staying curious and asking questions. Addressing Fear and Self-Doubt. Persevering to the End. Confidence Emerges.

Ann and Doug have always shared with Noah that he should always do his best. He doesn't have to be *the* best. He just needs to do *his* best and as long as he does his best, that's all they ever asked. Her son is a talented and gifted student. Many will say, then you have nothing to worry about. That is so far from the truth. All children and adults have their strengths and limitations.

Noah is amazing with numbers and great at math. He is more of a linear thinker. He likes multiple choice. Ann despises multiple choice. She over-thinks the question and the answers and then second guesses herself when making the final choice for the answer. Give her an essay question and she's a happy camper. Noah can figure things out in his head that Ann's lucky to do with a calculator. He remembers math problems from tests and the ones he got wrong. He used to tell her why he got it wrong and went through the entire problem.

He talked about a calculus equation once, looked at Ann after explaining it and said, "You have no idea what I'm talking about, do you?"

Ann simply said, "You lost me at Calculus."

They both laughed and understood she cared but didn't have a clue what he just said.

Noah is a perfectionist. Serves him well and paralyzes him at the same time.

The upside—he wants things to be right and takes time to get it right!

The downside—sometimes he takes *sooooo* much time agonizing over the many details and or feelings that he doesn't end up accomplishing what he wants!

During a particularly challenging semester at school, Noah had many papers to write. Give Noah a paper to write and can he write it? Yes. Does he do a good job? Yes. Is it a major challenge for him? Yes, because he works to have *each* and *every* word and sentence right the first time. Does it serve him well? Ann's not certain. She believes it would take less time to put the ideas on paper and go back and edit. It's hard for him to have the patience to write, read, revise, and repeat. Therefore, at times he puts off starting the paper until the eleventh hour. Then the stress sets in and he wonders if he has time to write the paper.

Neither style is right nor wrong. People have to do things the way they believe is best for them.

Ann's dad, who taught her a great deal, always said, "Do it right the first time so you don't have to do it again." There's a lot of truth to that statement; however, there's a time to do it right the first time and there may also be a time to exercise patience and to write, revise, revisit, and repeat until the finished product is the best it can be.

When Noah came to Ann and Doug and shared that he was stuck on a paper, one of the first things they did was to compliment him for having the courage to ask for help. Because let's face it—it's hard to ask for help, especially when you're in college and working to establish your independence. They assured him everybody gets stuck. They asked him lots of questions to gain a better understanding, not just for themselves, but to show him how he could get himself *unstuck* in the future. It's hard for your kids to ask for help. It's hard for most people to ask for help. Many times, for our kiddos, everything they see in their parents' or other people's lives is going well, when the successes and lessons may have taken years of work and lessons learned through the school of hard knocks. On the surface, it appears things are or have always been easy. They aren't privy to the past, which has influenced them and the obstacles they had to overcome to gain the wisdom of today.

Ann and Doug now share some struggles they had, and still have, with Noah so he can learn from his mistakes as well as theirs on how he can overcome his struggles. Granted, it's important to share with kids what's appropriate at the time and based on where they are in life.

Through asking him several questions without judgment and working to avoid the "why" questions because they can put people on the defensive, they discovered several things. One, he wasn't all that interested in writing the paper, because he didn't really like to write. Two, he couldn't see the relevance of the entire project as it related to him being successful in his career. Three, self-doubt and fear were present because he had worked himself into a tizzy and didn't know if he could write and organize the paper as it needed to be for the grade he wanted to earn. And four, he faced comparison— would it be as good as other papers written by his peers? He had even chosen the topic because it interested him. They assured him his feelings were completely normal. His parents wanted him to face his fears, not let them overpower or define his thoughts. They worked through the following steps:

One. Make a first decision whether to complete the class, as it was not required to graduate. While he didn't necessarily *want* to complete the class, he also didn't want to feel as if he had quit or to have regrets about not completing the paper. Decision made. He was going to finish the class perseverance and commitment). Proud parent moment.

Two. There are things in life you may not want to do yet need to do to get to your end goal. Here the feeling of completing what he started was important because growing up, the message he learned was, "you finish what you start." Granted, there may come a time in life when finishing a project doesn't make sense or a different path needs to be taken, but that's a different topic to be addressed at another time.

Three. Relevance to his career. This was about learning more regarding the process of research, working through difficult times, and finishing a project that would help with confidence and future projects in life. He also needed to prepare a poster to present at a research fair, which proved to be an additional challenge. One that Noah met and completed by designing a poster that was easy to read and was packed full of interesting and thought-provoking information.

Four. They worked to assure him the journey and what he learned along the way was by far more important at that point than the grade or what the others did for their project. Easy for parents to say—they weren't presenting a research poster with a group of peers. They asked what it would take to earn the grade he wanted and feel good about his poster. He developed an action plan that included meeting on a more regular basis with his professor who oversaw his Honors project, checking in with his parents and himself from time to time, double checking the requirements for the paper and poster, and using a calendar. You might think this sounded easy or unnecessary. It's important to note this was also during the pandemic, which affected everyone in different ways. Everyone experienced the pandemic differently, depending on their age and stage of life. That, too, is a topic for another time and place.

Long story short? He addressed his fears, allowed others to share insight with him, and overcame his own fears and self-doubt. He finished the paper and project and worked through every challenge and obstacle which got in his way. Ann and Doug asked him after graduation what grade he earned. He shared that he earned an A. They congratulated him and assured him that while the A was awesome, the greatest accomplishment was not in the grade earned; it was *what he learned*. The journey and lessons learned and not the destination (the grade) was what he will take with him when he or a peer encounters a similar challenge in life.

Lessons Learned

- Wisdom can be the voice of reason.

- Wisdom is learned through experiences.

- Nobody knows everything about anything.

- You know more than you think you do. The trick is recognizing how much you've learned and knowing when to use the wisdom you've gained.

- You can learn from the experiences and wisdom of others.

- FAIL actually stands for 'First Attempt In Learning.' A mistake is only a failure if you fail to learn from it. Mistakes are merely learning opportunities. They happen every day.

- Mistakes are inevitable and are learning opportunities.

- There's always something new you can learn, and everyone has something to share, no matter how old or young. If you have not walked in someone's shoes, don't say you know how they feel. You don't. You may understand the emotion and even know what sadness, loss, or joy feels like; however, all experiences are unique. Losing a spouse through divorce is not the same as losing them through death. Both are losses, yet the losses are through different circumstances.

- People come in and out of our lives for different reasons and in different seasons of our lives. Some stay for a long time, others for a short time, others are there just not physically present. You can't see them, but you know they're there, just like the elephant.

My Strength

- I give you the opportunity to apply all the things you've learned throughout the years, perhaps saving you some anguish, and hopefully not making the same mistake again.

Your Strengths (List the strengths you see in yourself when it comes to recognizing the wisdom you've acquired.)

Strategies: Choose the one(s) which will best serve you.

- Keep learning.

- Ask questions.

- Use the knowledge you have.

- Read.

- Take a class.

- Look at mistakes as learning opportunities.
- Try new things.
- Ask yourself what you've learned through each experience.
- Use experiences and mistakes as learning opportunities.

Your Reflection

Reflection Questions: Answer here or in a separate journal.

1. What are some of the biggest lessons I've learned through my mistakes?
2. How can I share what I've learned in a positive and caring manner with others?

What wisdom have I acquired throughout the years?Your Biggest Take-away(s) Regarding Wisdom

Your Action Plan

Here is an example of what your action plan may look like. Remember it's your plan not mine, this is only an example to support you in getting started. Choose the action which will support you in moving forward. There is space for you to write your personal plan of action at the end of the example.

1. *Goal: Journal and track what I have learned from my mistakes.*
2. *Action: With each milestone or experience as well as mistakes made I will ask myself, "What can I learn from this experience?" And if a mistake is made or something has gone awry ask, "How can I prevent it from happening again?"*

3. *Who will support me? Husband, friend, colleagues.*

4. *Date: Begin September 3rd. Going to do this weekly.*

5. *How will I know I'm making progress? Weekly conversations with my husband and I will consciously use what I have learned.*

Your Turn: Answer here or in a separate journal.

1. Goal:

2. Action:

3. Who can support you?

4. Date to begin:

5. How will you know you made progress?

Thanks for hanging out and taking time to meet my friends and me. I encourage you to continue and read the conclusion as well as complete the activities at the end of the book. Enjoy the journey.

Additional Resources

- *C. S. Lewis' Little Book of Wisdom: Meditations on Faith, Life, Love, and Literature* By C. S. Lewis, Andrea Kirk Assaf, et al.

- *In Search of Wisdom: Life-Changing Truths in the Book of Proverbs* by Joyce Meyer.

- TEDx talk "Closing the gap between knowledge and wisdom" by Vanessa Adams.

Conclusion

The End or is it Really the Beginning?

"The secret of getting ahead is getting started. The secret to getting started is breaking your overwhelming tasks into small manageable tasks and then starting on the first one."

Mark Twain

*T*hanks for taking time to meet our team members, your team within, and allowing each of us to share the role we play in your journey. Our common purpose is to serve and support you in being successful. We're going to let Ann take over from here with the conclusion.

ℐ ℐ ℐ

Thanks for letting my "friends" share their insights into leading your team within. It's my hope you've enjoyed learning a little more about the team that lives within each of us and had some fun along the way. I am reminded of my husband's favorite movie, *The Breakfast Club*. Five students who could not be more different, or so they thought based on their own appearance, judgments, and biases, end up in an all-day Saturday detention. They found a common purpose, surviving Saturday, and became friends for at least the day.

Your team is similar to the students. They're all different yet have a common purpose; to support you in becoming the best version of yourself you can be. Will they spend just one day together, or will you let them acknowledge each other and work together throughout your entire journey? Deep within all of us lies our team, the Butterfly, the Cat, the Dove, the Eagle, the Elephant, the Monkey, the Ostrich, the Owl, the Parrot, the Puppy, the Rabbit, the Sloth, the Snake, the Squirrel, the Tortoise, and of course, the Geese. I'm still helping them work together, as well as allowing them to work their magic on their own, giving them the spotlight when they need to use their own unique qualities to help me be the best leader I can be.

What will you do? Will you lead your team within and help it grow to support you in living the life you want and are meant to live? Will you help your peers in learning to lead themselves and their internal and external teams? There are a couple of activities at the end of the book meant to support you as you continue this journey to lead your team within.

Together, along with our experiences, our knowledge, our desires, and that which we want and are meant to be, they provide us with the foundation to build the life we were meant to live.

Things don't always turn out like we want or think they should. However, I am reminded of one of my favorite quotes by Joseph Campbell, "We must let go of the life we have planned so as to accept the one that is waiting for us." There's a world of opportunity just waiting for you as you lead the team within and allow their strengths to become yours and live the life you're meant to live.

Here are a few of the overall lessons I've learned and what I like most about each of my team members.

Lessons Learned

- Take time to enjoy the journey every step of the way.

- Beauty is in the eye of the beholder. It's not only how we appear on the outside, it's how we feel, and see ourselves from the inside, which contributes to our self-confidence and worth.

- Appreciate each team member and season of life. Respect what each of your team members brings to the table, at work and in your personal life.

- Enjoy each moment because it really is a gift.

- Enjoy everyone who comes in and out of your life. Learn from them. Share with them.

- Life is like a jigsaw puzzle. There are many pieces, just like there are many team members who bring unique qualities to the team. They all fit together. Start with one goal, like putting the border together first or establishing the foundation of your team. All the team members will find their place and contribute to the team. The result? A beautiful picture. A successful team. Does it take time? Yes, but my dad used to tell me, "Anything worth having is worth working for." I think he was right.

- Everyone is a leader in their own way. You don't need a title. You just need the desire to lead and the ability to listen to your team.

- Find what is important to you and your peers, and then keep going until you achieve your goal. Think about what would have happened if the butterfly stopped just before it broke through that last layer of the cocoon? Are you stopping just before you turn the corner of where your dreams and goals are waiting for you?

- Motivation comes from within. We can inspire people; however, each person has to find their own motivation deep within themselves. People do things for their reasons, not yours.

By the way—Some of you may wonder why the lion on the cover doesn't have a chapter. The lion is you. It represents the strength and courage you had to buy and read this book in order to become more self-aware of how you can continue to grow into the leader you want to be, and explore what actions you will decide to take to support you in effectively leading the team you hold within yourself. You are the lion, the creator and leader of your team and your own destiny.

What I like most about what each animal has taught me and brings to my life.

I have truly discovered an appreciation for each of the animals and how they support me in creating the best version of myself. While I admire all their traits, listed below are some of the characteristics I admire most. There's also a place at the end of the book for you to list what characteristic(s) you have come to admire or appreciate the most in each team member.

The Geese: It's important to recognize the value each team member brings to the team and to me.

The Butterfly: Change is inevitable and the transformation that can take place is worth the time and effort of working through all the changes. In the end it all works out the way it's supposed to and many times can be even better than we imagined.

The Cat: Asking questions with a curious mind opens up so many more possibilities than I ever imagined. The "what" questions help people feel more comfortable and can help all of us dig deeper and experience more meaningful conversations.

The Dove: Finding inner peace is being grateful and enjoying what I have.

The Eagle: I am enough and am stronger than I thought.

The Elephant: Conversations are crucial to have and when approached with kindness and compassion they aren't as uncomfortable as we think they're going to be. Anticipation of the conversation is usually far worse than the conversation itself.

The Monkey: I have the opportunity to explore the underlying reason I'm putting off doing what I think or know I'm supposed to be working on.

The Ostrich: Focusing on one thing at a time can help me make more forward progress than multi-tasking or trying to accomplish too many goals at the same time.

The Parrot: What I say to myself impacts my thoughts, actions, and self-confidence. I can control my self-talk, and it does make a difference what I say to myself.

The Puppy: Take time to do things which bring me joy and laugh often. I will be more relaxed and productive if I take time for myself.

The Rabbit: While I have many choices in which dream(s) to pursue, it's best to focus on one until I'm successful.

The Sloth: Slowing down doesn't mean slacking off. It means I may need to slow down, take a breath or two, so I am able to reflect and reevaluate things. Sometimes slowing down can actually help me speed up.

The Snake: Don't compare myself to others. The grass isn't greener on the other side. It's just a different shade of green.

The Squirrel: I have the ability to decide what interruptions are important and respond to them and that I am, at times, my own interruption.

The Tortoise: Stay the course if it's important to you. The race isn't always won by the swiftest but truly by those who keep on running.

The Owl: Wisdom is found in all kinds of experiences.

Thanks again for hanging out with my team members and me. Discover what works *best for you*. Remember—You have a wealth of talent and much to offer the world. ***Lead your team and enjoy the journey!***

May each of you follow your dreams and accomplish the goals which are important to you.

Ann

This isn't the end – it really is just the beginning.

What do you like most about what each of the animals teaches you and brings to your life?

The Geese:

The Butterfly:

The Cat:

The Dove:

The Eagle:

The Elephant:

The Monkey:

The Ostrich:

The Parrot:

The Puppy:

The Rabbit:

The Sloth:

The Snake:

The Squirrel:

The Tortoise:

The Owl:

Self-Assessment as
You Continue to Move Forward

*T*his is an opportunity for you to reflect on the progress you've made as you implement strategies from the book or those which you discover on your own.

Once you determine which area you're most challenged with, go back to the chapter in question and make your action plan and decide which steps you're going to take to elevate and manage that particular skill.

Feel free to re-assess yourself based on where you see yourself now that you've worked on an area. A copy of the self-assessment can be found on the next page.(1 - I could still use some work on this but am getting better all the time. 2 - Sometimes I have it and sometimes I don't. 3 - I got this.)

Each of us is a leader regardless of whether we have a title that refers to leadership. You neither have to be in the lead to be the leader, nor do you have to be the leader to lead.

Characteristic	Check which one you're working on	Progress Made
I can **lead** in situations when appropriate. (Geese)		1 2 3
I am comfortable and **able to follow** someone's lead. (Geese)		1 2 3
I am **able to collaborate** with others. (Geese)		1 2 3
I **accept change** for the most part. (Butterfly)		1 2 3
I am **curious and ask questions.** (Cat)		1 2 3
I am a **patient** person. (Cat)		1 2 3
I am good at **self-care.** (Cat)		1 2 3
I experience **inner peace.** (Dove)		1 2 3
I feel **confident** in most things and in most situations. (Eagle)		1 2 3
I am **able to communicate** with most people. (Elephant)		1 2 3
I am able to **address conflict** in a productive manner. (Elephant)		1 2 3
I have **procrastination** under control. (Monkey)		1 2 3
I am **able to focus** on my priorities/projects. (Ostrich)		1 2 3
I **do not avoid** things that are uncomfortable. (Ostrich)		1 2 3
My **self-tal**k is usually positive and serves me well. (Parrot)		1 2 3
I **laugh** and have fun. (Puppy)		1 2 3
I am **loyal**. (Puppy)		1 2 3
I take time to **relax**. (Puppy)		1 2 3
I am able to **make decisions** on what my **priorities** are. (Rabbit)		1 2 3
I am able to **slow down** when appropriate. (Sloth)		1 2 3
I **don't compare** myself to others. (Snake)		1 2 3
I **don't allow fear** to stop me from doing things. (Snake)		1 2 3
I am able to manage my **self-doubt.** (Snake)		1 2 3
I am **not easily distracted.** (Squirrel)		1 2 3
I **manage interruptions.** (Squirrel)		1 2 3
I **persevere** during tough situations. (Tortoise)		1 2 3
I am a **patient** person. (Tortoise)		1 2 3
I gain **wisdom** from mistakes and experiences. (Owl)		1 2 3

The Windshield and the Rearview Mirror

"Inner peace is knowing you have balance in your life and are investing time in a variety of areas. No one thing should ever be your whole life. For if it were taken away, where would you be?"

Ann Wright

Seven-Step Process for Achieving Balance

This is an exercise you can complete to support you in thinking about what you want to achieve and how to balance your time so you can focus on it. Choose whatever area you want to in life (career/day at work, a project, personal life) and begin working through the steps. Some like to use the word harmony or alignment. BALANCE works for the steps; however, choose what word resonates with you.

1. Begin with a vision: What is a goal you want to achieve or what area of life needs a little more balance. Don't worry about the "how." That will be revealed later in the process.

2. Assess where you are spending your time: I spend my time doing the following (be honest):

Activity   Time spent on it

_____   _____

_____   _____

_____   _____

_____   _____

3. Listen to your heart and list your priorities: List your priorities. You can always go back and put them in order of priority. You can re-prioritize them in the future based on life's changes.

My Priorities

_____   _____   _____

_____   _____   _____

_____   _____   _____

4. Analyze and take action: Based upon your priorities, where you're spending your time, and where you want to spend your time, where is your time being spent that it shouldn't be? Where do you want/need to spend your time?

_____   _____   _____

_____   _____   _____

_____   _____   _____

5. Negotiate: What activities and with whom will you negotiate in order to take action and make time to achieve your goal?

Activity which needs to be negotiated	Person with whom I need to negotiate

6. Change: I commit to making the following changes. You may want to determine the change(s) you want to work on before you decide with whom to negotiate.

Change to be made	Date by when the change will be made

7. Evaluate and enjoy: List the change made and how it's working for you. List with whom you want to celebrate and how.

The change made	Is it working for me? If yes, great; if no, what will I change?	With whom will I celebrate?

Life is a juggling act: make time for what matters most.

Acknowledgements

This book is a reality because of the unwavering support of many people. My apologies as I was not able to list everyone by name who supported me throughout this journey.

Thanks to Doug, my husband, who continues to believe in me and supports me in all of my many ideas and journeys, especially in writing this book. I'm not certain who is happier to see it finally finished, him or me! I'm sure there were plenty of times when he grew tired of hearing me say that I wanted to write a book. But it's finally done—it's written!

Thanks to Noah, the only one in the world who calls me 'Mom.' His matter-of-fact "just do it" attitude helped me more than he will ever know. I can't wait to write the next book in collaboration with him!

Thanks to my mom, who guides me every day, and to my dad, who watches over me each day from above, and who supported me through thick and thin and taught me more than I can say. My dad shared his business sense. My mom shared her heart and compassion.

Thanks to my sisters. Cindi provided inspiration and prayers, especially through the self-doubt days. Susan is a great example of how to persevere in tough times. I am thankful for her insight.

Thank you to my mentors and friends who continued to encourage me to find the strength to finish this. To my Jaycee and lifelong friends—joining the Jaycees was undoubtedly one of the best decisions I have ever made. I met many of my friends through the Jaycees and we are friends, not because we're Jaycees, but because we share common bonds and still live by our creed, especially the last line of it which states "Service to humanity is the *BEST* work of life."

Thank you to my girlfriends—it's true. Boyfriends may come and go, but girlfriends last forever. Special thanks to Shelley; you are always there to lend a listening ear, and to Marci, for sharing your honest opinion when you knew how hard it was for me to share that first chapter.

To Christi Hegstad and the entire ASPIRE team, who never gave me grief for setting the same Bold Goal year after year until it finally came to fruition.

To Mitch Mathews and the entire Acceleration team who provided a community of support, especially during the pandemic, when I needed a community to lean on and kick me in the backside when you knew I needed it.

To everyone at Self-Publishing and my Coaches Kerk Murray and Andrew Biernet—the two of you helped me make a long-time dream come true.

Thank you to all who provided stories and strategies: Aree Bly, Deanna Cavin, Janet Fisher, Joe Van Haecke, Lynn McGrane Kuhn, Julie Richards, Lisa Swanepole, Kevin Urban, and Alison Vandry.

Most of all, I thank God for all the blessings in life. They truly come from his grace. Faith makes things possible, not always easy.

Peace and blessings,

Ann

I'd love to Connect!

Thank you so much for deciding to invest in yourself and allowing me to walk this journey with you. To say thanks, please visit my website at www.annwrightsolutions.com/freegift to receive your gift, a worksheet to support you in moving forward with your dreams and goals.

Got Advice for Our College Grads?

If you would like to provide some advice or tips in being successful in life for new or recent college graduates, please go to www.annwrightsolutions.com/advice to share your thoughts. You will receive credit for your contribution if they are included in my next book which will be written in collaboration with my son.

About Ann Wright

$\mathcal{A}$nn is the founder of The Wright Coaching and Training Solutions. What she would love to see more of in the world is this: more people who believe in themselves and recognize the gifts and talents they bring to the world as well as appreciate the talent others bring.

Throughout Ann's 25 plus years of experience in leadership and talent development she discovered and believes that people are an organization's most valuable asset. She partners with organizations and leaders to achieve their personal and professional goals by focusing on people, culture, and everyone's unique talents. She is comfortable asking tough questions with kindness and compassion. Together they discover where they are, where they want to be, and what they are willing and able to do to achieve their goals. Ann believes businesses thrive by investing in their team members and embracing the talent each brings. Through coaching and workshops, Ann helps people develop their skills and reach their goals. She is a certified leadership and team coach with a master's degree in business leadership.

Ann lives with her husband in Ankeny, IA. They have one adult son. She enjoys spending time with family and friends and is an active volunteer in her community. Some of her favorite volunteer activities include volunteering at her church, and being a member of Rotary, the local chamber, and the Iowa chapter of the International Coaching Federation.

www.ingramcontent.com/pod-product-compliance
Lightning Source LLC
Chambersburg PA
CBHW061817040426
42447CB00012B/2697